MW01136966

The

Pleiadian

Child

Carol Ann

Noonan

Readers reviews for The Pleiadian Child

"Stumbled on this book by chance and decided to give it a go not expecting much. But...it exceeded my expectations. First part is a description of the authors rough life story mixed with her psychic gifts experiences. Other half she channels Pleiadians and their messages that I found to be highly interesting and eye-opening. Ended up finishing this book quite quick due to it's compelling information."

Marcus White

"Mesmerizing. From the depths of a terrible childhood to the strong spiritual woman she is today, she takes us on an incredible journey."

Lynda

Contents

Acknowledgements

I dedicate this book to all the Indigo, Crystal and Rainbow children, those that came before them and those that will come after them. To my family, we live and learn. To all the others out there living on earth, who are waking up and remembering who you are, you are "Star Children". To all those who are now also remembering The Pleiadians/Star Nations as children. Wake up and step up and out into the world with your voice strong, your head high, you are not alone in your childhood memories of The Pleiadians/Star Nations. We are not alone, we have never been alone. I would like to give thanks to all people listed here they have all helped me in their own way. Some of them are good friends. Some of them I haven't met, yet, but they have all been my most important teachers.

Mark, Lee, Mum, Granddad, Kerry.

For all of my family, lest they should ever forget the truth

Jimmy Delaney

Family of Light

Kiesha Crowther, Drunvalo Melchizedek, Doreen Virtue, Neale Donald Walsch, Ken Carey, Ted Andrews.

Mary Queeney, Mary Ann Summer Rain, Amorah Quan Yin.

The Pleiadians, Jesus, All of my Ancestors, My Guides.

Paul O'Halloran & Melanie Gomes.

Joshua Shapiro & Katrina Head.

Emma & Vivian, Caroline O'Donovan.

Derek McGowan, Patrick Justin Lee.

Wayne Herschel.

Caroline & Reg Ellis.

Eric Von Daniken.

To my partner, my lover, my best friend, my twin flame, my whole package. Thank you for believing in me when doubt crept in, for seeing that I was never that little girl they said I was. For your endless time, patience and understanding. For the way you love me.

I love you to the ends of the earth and to the heart of the Pleiades. J.A.

Foreword

All I'd ever wanted was to be "normal" for such a long time, what seemed to me like a lifetime, a sentence of being different, not something seen, but rather something felt by others and myself. Spiritually, I was so different and for many, many years I longed and ached to fit in and be "normal". My spiritual gift saved my life at the age of twelve; of that, there is no doubt for me. My childhood years were besieged with abuse of all kinds which came at me from many different places, with men lurking in the darkest of corners, often literally while they abused me. I remained transfixed on the light, the light of the spiritual worlds and dimensions and travelled way out of my body and connected with the Pleiadians.

My childhood years were difficult, to say the least. I was abused, raped, neglected and starved. But it was because of this that my path to the spiritual worlds opened up, "really opened up". I learnt much and received many gifts of experience. Premonitions were a common thing. I spent most of my childhood half in this world and half in the spirit world.

At the age of seventeen, I would wake up to watch "my dream" in the morning, on the news. To say it scared me is putting it mildly but over the years, it was a process that I learned to deal with, to the point I've been able to work with and help the police and families, often in tragic circumstances. My gifts have often felt like a curse at times. It is experience that comes with knowing that it is a gift, to be able to help, even in the tragic cases I often have to deal with.

But all I ever wanted to be was "normal". I'm laughing, as I write these words because I'm much further from "normal" now than I ever was. Today, I'm happy, very happy with who I am. But I ached to be "normal". It was never gonna happen, not even with my birth, nor "any" part of my childhood, nor my schooling, nor my parents, nor the abuse. All of it led me on to the spiritual path, which was even less "normal".

Today, I try and use all of my gifts and abilities to the best of my ability to help people. I no longer confine myself to "psychic" or "medium" or "healer". My path is more of the Shaman.

I remember countless past lives and I've shared a few with you in this book. But there are many more. My story is a unique one that I hope you gain some comfort, wisdom, and knowledge from. I hope it gives you peace and hope and connects you to your own awareness, consciousness, and expansion of the truth of our shared history. Our ancestors, your ancestors, my ancestors, we are all connected, like the thread on a web, we are not limited to this planet, far from it, (no pun intended). Our roots lie out in the universe, our history began far from earth and we are not alone. We have never been alone.

These days, when I connect with the Pleiadians they are much like "Archangels" energy wise and we have nothing to fear. I believe that everything that exists has an opposite, as above so below, yin and yang. Something cannot exist in the universe without it having an opposite. Our awareness on earth, as part of humanity, is shifting and expanding. We are part of the Ascension and the star nations are here to help us to wake up, remember who we are, who you are.

Summer

"Summer it comes and goes
Just like the leaves on the trees
Just like the rain and snow
Just like the Summer and Winter
But better in Oh so many ways"

Karma and The Stars

We lay silently on the ground beneath the night sky in the darkness, stillness surrounding us. A hazy peace fell over us. We lay down on an Island in the middle of the ocean; few words were needed between us, as we connected with each other in silence and gazed upon the night sky in awe. The closer we became in the silence, the more peaceful we lay side by side. Gazing up, we watched the night sky and stars above us like a blanket. There were no clouds, no light pollution to be seen, just a brilliantly crystal clear night Sky, so beautifully laid out above us, as far as our eyes could see.

And then it happened. One of the *"Stars"* moved, I gasped, but neither of us spoke, not wanting to break the stillness, the peace of the night. My eyes fixated on to the *"Star"* that moved in a pattern, in amazement at what was occurring in the universe. I couldn't take my eyes off it as it moved around the night sky in a rhythmic pattern for all to see. Neither of us dared to break the silence or speak the words of truth of what we had both seen, witnessed together, but we both knew that it wasn't a *"Star"* that moved that night. Neither of us ever spoke of this to each other. I left Holy Island a few months later, not knowing

where my journey would take me. At the time, I
had little knowledge of The Pleiadians or other
Star Nations and no insight into a connection with
The Pleiadians.

Holy Island, Scotland, 2004

The First Flight Out

He lay on top of me crushing my body, my young seemingly weightless body. I could barely breathe as I lay gasping for air. His body was so heavy that I couldn't move. The stink of whiskey on his breath, that memory will never leave me. Painfully and sadly, it haunts me still. Any hint of a smell of whiskey always takes me right back to that first moment, that I consciously and fully remember. That is probably why I have always hated the smell of whiskey, along with my mum's long, long, addiction to it and other alcohol. Her own smell of whiskey, that seemed to forever linger from her own pores and body, must have been a constant reminder to me, all the way during my childhood years. No wonder I longed to escape the home we all lived in. His force was strong and heavy like a dead weight on top of me. I was slowly being crushed (somewhere along the years, I developed a fear of enclosed spaces and claustrophobia and the link is very obvious to me, now) His body lay rigid, his full weight on top of me, my body felt it would simply collapse and disintegrate into the floor beneath me. I was in the centre of my room with no escape, I couldn't breathe. Then it happened my first flight out, away from Bill. With what seemed like a snap of the fingers, I left my body, The Pleiadians connected with me;

"Just breathe, just wait, this moment will pass in less than a second you will be safe. We are your family and we love you, we are watching over you. We know your journey will be much more difficult than most and easier than some. Have patience and wait. You came from here once and it's here you shall return, upon your own physical death, you shall greet us and we you. We love you more than words can express. We are family. The Universe is vast and there is no place in the universe where energy does not exist. Stars, planets, galaxies, All contain life in one form or another. All is energy and no-thing is separate from any other thing. All is connected, All is one, even the creator, God, source energy or whatever word you choose to use. We Love you, we are always with you, we are blood family, we will be waiting for you when your body dies. Our connection will never, ever cease. *Now go back* into your body".

Again, with what seemed like a snap of the fingers, I was back in my body, gasping for air and trying to avoid his mouth, I kept turning my head from side to side or, at least, I did my very best trying to turn my head. His hand reached up to force my head and mouth still. No escape, like a deer caught in the headlights. I couldn't move and there seemed to be no escape for me. Somehow, I knew what was to come, either instinctively, intuitively or telepathically. Looking back, I believe it must have been telepathically, I read his mind. I could see the image in his mind clear as day, of what he was wanting to do to my body, though I was only eight and didn't yet know anything at all about sex. I saw what he was going to do and some part of me felt the pain of it in my body like It was being ripped to shreds internally but it was just an image.

I felt the door open from behind me, my brother's voice loud, clear and strong. He was there to save me from being raped and all the pain, emotionally and physically, of that. My brother effortlessly lifted the man by the collar, who was crushing me, as if he was as light as a feather or two. All the while he just kept repeating "What are you doing? What are you doing?". His voice sounded kind of strangled, tormented, violated, angry, strong, hateful, forceful so very loving and protective of me as if he would go to the ends of the earth to protect me and I knew he would and has done so many times. My brother not bothering, caring or listening to what the man was saying, doing or his reactions started to hit him, violently. I lay there in stillness regaining my breath and with the air around me again, that I could again breathe easily. My brother continued to hit him and hit him. I could hear or sense my mum making her way towards us, in the long, long hallway that we had. She must have heard the sounds, noise and sensed the violence. She entered the room and quickly, only seeing my brother's violence, lunged herself at my brother, trying to protect Bill, not at all realising what had just happened and the reason behind my brother's violence. I don't think she even saw me lying on the floor.

In 2012 I began my Shamanic course in Galway, it was during one of these weekends while in an Altered state of awareness that I fully remembered that memory, thankfully and I know there is more to come, that more of my memories will re-surface and be shared with you in this book.

"We are such stuff that dreams are made of"

The Maltese Falcon

The Early Years

Chapter 1

Age Seven

Ireland: A New Land

We left Namibia, got on a plane and landed in
Ireland somewhere probably Dublin. My mum,
brother, sister and I we were heading to my
grandparent's home. I'd never met them before
and was feeling quite curious about them. There
was also a sense of trepidation and uncertainty. I
believe we all felt this. My mum had finally
decided to officially separate, after many years of
living what *must have been* a very unhappy life
for her. My father was *very* abusive. I've heard
many stories over the years, one, in particular, is
so cruel. I'd heard from my sister mostly that
there was one time that he'd arrived home drunk
yet again. In the morning took a dislike to
something and began to get violent and abusive.
As anyone who has ever met, known, or been in
an abusive relationship will know, the abusers
can be the nicest, kind-hearted and caring people
at times, especially in public - the proverbial
"street angel, house devil". Outside our kitchen
door that led to the garden and clothesline, was a
couple of stones steps or maybe they were
concrete but either way, he had my mum on the
floor and was banging her head on to the steps.
It makes me feel sick to think of it and how cruel
he was and must have been to her. So she had

finally decided to leave him and head for her
Ireland after many years, twenty, thirty years?

Granddad

My Granddad and I were very close right from the
very beginning. I had a huge connection to him,
a bond that has never broken, even in his death.
I was born in Namibia, South West Africa. I think
it was in 1979 at the age of five that we left. We
boarded the air plane bound for Ireland, where
my mum was born and bred. Being a good
Catholic at heart, she had an enormously difficult
time due to her divorce and spent many years
battling her own demons and the views of The
Catholic Church regarding "divorce", as this was
not her choice, I'm told but her husband's final
decision so that was that. And so I meet my
Granddad in 1979 at his home village in Partry, a
small village in County Mayo where he grew up,
as many of his relations before him had, the land
being passed down from generation to generation
on the male side.

We had travelled a long way and spent a good

few days travelling to get to him. The land was lush and green and there was so much of it, or so it seemed to me as a five-year-old. I fondly remember playing out in the garden, during the summers. During these years the winters were magical to me, I spent long evenings curled up in my granddad's lap in front of the fire, warm and cared for, with his telling me stories, tales, and fables of all kinds, some true and some not. We had a huge bond with each other, right from the very beginning. And I will always love him. He was a kind, soft gentleman and he was well liked by all, a good Catholic and not just the Sunday type. In 1988, he passed away, surrounded by all of his family and me, in the Sacred Heart Hospital in Castlebar. It was an experience I will never forget. Little did I know that it would be a catalyst for my spiritual path, that I now found myself fully engaged in and have been *ever since* then.

Dublin, Oh Sweet Dublin, Remembered

My mum and I went visiting Dublin, away from our temporary home at the time. My mum is Irish and her roots go back a very long way. We lived with my grandparents, in their tiny little cottage. Idyllic and postcard perfect, all except for the cold Winter months, when the frosty ice and wind would try and eat your skin alive. If you had money, you had warmth, fire, warm clothes and protection from the Winter months. We never had either which left us open and cold in the Winter. I will always remember how I was so cold on a daily basis during my childhood. There was no way to get warm, except to run and play outside, with or without other kids. I just hated the cold and still do, I can't abide it.

We were visiting Dublin, I must have been about seven I guess. It was my first time there, except I remembered it from a previous life. I was looking up at the tall wide buildings and the more I looked at them, the more I started to remember a previous lifetime. When I was a man and lived and worked in Dublin. I was a happily married family man, with two or three children and a loving wife. I started to tell my mum and started to show her where things were such as buildings, places, place names etc., and how the local area used to be in days gone by. Now, she obviously knew that I hadn't been there before, in this lifetime anyway. She certainly would have known about it. Looking back, I do find it ever so strange that on so many occasions on this one, especially, she never asked me any questions. But I'm sure now, it was mostly out of fear, mostly fear for me. I mean I was telling her what buildings were around the corner and facts that she could see with her own eyes. I have since been told by my spirit guides that she never asked me because of her own fear, with regards to anything psychic. She herself is very psychic and has an enormous amount of fear and this fear has held her back. Not only has it held her back, it has really been to her detriment because this is largely why she has been an alcoholic for most of her life and that is incredibly sad and tragic, I think. So there I was remembering a past life at about the age of seven and telling her what I was seeing and remembering, including the buildings and my life as a happily married family man. I was involved with the church but was more spiritual, than religious, wanting to do the best for the people in my community. I was very high up in my career and successful. I owned a factory or two that made clothes. I was a much liked and well-respected Gentleman who had a lot of compassion for his workforce and was much liked in the community. I had little stress and dealt with problems as they arose calmly and compassionately, very much a people person, caring about each individual on a personal basis. I myself had few problems and took everything in my stride, sincere and easy to get on with. Almost everything I was remembering came to me very quickly in images and feelings which came to me in a matter of a few moments. My mum never questioned me about this memory I was having but I was happy on this occasion to tell her what I was experiencing. I think she rather didn't want to know or even to hear what I was saying. Her fear has largely caused her to dismiss much of what I did share with her as a child, but there was so much more that I didn't tell her and, unfortunately, I was probably right to not do so.

The Sound of Peacocks

Vague distant memories of my childhood occasionally haunt me at times, as if my mind wants to remember. Then realises that it doesn't want to remember. Then the memory is gone. My mum was sober for a while, at least for a good few months. Living in Dublin, she had a job as a cook in the zoo. Life was really peaceful and full of the sound of peacocks and other animals, but mostly peacocks. We used to take a small boat through parts of the zoo, through quiet wilderness and trees. Magnificent scenery and nature surrounded us with beautiful sounds. It was very peaceful. We were living in accommodation provided by the zoo and, therefore, it wasn't of a very good quality. I don't remember where my brother and sister were at this time but, looking back, it seems they were living in Falmouth with their dad. I developed a cough that turned serious. The doctor suggested it was due to all the damp at the accommodation. It was a real shame, I didn't want to leave Dublin, any more than my mum did, but still, we moved, I believe, back to England.

So the peaceful tranquillity and being sober all came to a quick, reluctant and abrupt end for both of us. I felt it was partly because my mum didn't seem to know what to do with herself, she didn't know how to live her life sober. She longed to escape from the mundane.

Unspoken words lay between us and hung in the air creating a distance that grew between us over the years. She blamed me for getting ill, not intentionally, but we both seemed to know what leaving the zoo would mean. It would bring a return of her drinking and, for that, she blamed me. At least, that's what I felt. I felt responsible for us having to leave and I felt responsible for her drinking again. The unspoken words between us created a gap that grew wider each year. As I got older, the distance grew and the more abuse I went through the more it grew wider and wider until eventually there seemed to be nothing left at all. My mum became like a stranger to me, I had no idea who she was. Yes, I knew she drank, but apart from that, I didn't even know who she really was, underneath that mask. Between the ages of about sixteen and twenty-six, I barely spoke to her.

So we moved from the zoo to London (if my memory serves me correctly). We lived in a B&B, all of us together, for about a year, until eventually we were offered a council flat in Hackney. Oh, the joy of it all. It really was bloody awful. My brother and sister were living with us at this time. As there were four of us, we were given a kind of large flat, at least, I thought so at the time. When I compared it to my grannies little cottage in Ireland, it was huge and on the fifth floor. A lot of decorating needed to be done but it was a start. My oldest brother even came to help us and we all were very glad to be out of the cramped B&B. My mum had no idea about decorating so thankfully my two brothers put themselves in charge. We ended up with artex on the lounge walls. It was razor sharp and God help you, if you touched it or knocked your arm against it, which I seemed to be forever doing, it really hurt and was sure to cut you and

31

draw blood, it was not a very good job.

My mum soon became a real hoarder, or maybe she always was. Items soon piled up over the years, we even had a parachute in the boiler cupboard. Maybe she was planning to go and do some jumps! The flat in the end was an awful mess of filth. Cleaning was never considered. It's very sad to think about it now, how she just drank her life away. She could have done so much, as so many other people could. Rarely did we have people back as we were all too ashamed. We often made attempts to clean it all up but you couldn't argue with my mum, it was her way or the highway. She never, ever chucked anything away and was always collecting things, along with not ever cleaning. Well you can imagine, we had eight TVs collected over the years, none of them bought, and all defective - one had sound, one had a picture, if we had two or three of them on all at the same time, we may have just about got to watch a program and be able to make sense of it. Wardrobes were put inside the front door; the house was crammed packed, full of junk and rubbish. There was nowhere else to put them. Looking back, it's still not funny and at the time it was utterly disgusting. We were living in filth. Stuff was piled high with barely any floor space. Clothes, furniture, magazines, books, newspapers, suitcases, boxes, chairs, the house was crammed with junk. To say it was filthy is an understatement. The kitchen was worst of all. Everything was covered with layers of dirt and grime. The dishes were rarely done, we even had bluebottle flies. It really was disgusting. The smell was the worst of it for me, as it clung to the back of my throat. I guess it's because of this that I have developed an overly healthy approach to having a clean house almost in a military fashion, which is a good thing having seen the opposite extreme. I also developed OCD and I can well link the two together if things are messy or dirty. I sometimes cannot even think straight and everything has to be in its *right place*, clean and modern or else I cannot function, I cannot think well. My brother is the same he simply cannot stand it either.

Having our windows cleaned one day, the guys in their lifts were on the outside of the building. I could hear them talking. I was in my mum's room lying on top of a mountain of her clothes, on top of the bed. I was hidden from sight buried amongst the clothes. I could hear them saying how disgusting it was and they asked how could people live like that? It was then that I realised just how bad the flat was, that this wasn't normal but extreme. And I longed for cleanliness. It also opened my eyes more to my mum's problem of being a hoarder. You can be a hoarder and clean but we were living in filth and it quite literally stank.

Drinking was my mum's world and being so young she didn't know what to do with me. I still remember the first time I saw snow, which was up to my waist. Being born in Southern Africa I hadn't seen snow before and we had recently moved to London. We were on the way to the local pub less than five minutes from our new flat. We were wading through the snow, with my mum half dragging me, so eager was she to get to the pub and escape her life of sorrows. Without a coat I was freezing I had been left outside in the doorway. I was too young to be allowed in, so I just wasn't. I stood there waiting for her like she told me to for hours at a time and it became a constant event, coat or no coat. My mum was lost in her own self-obsessed drunken stupor. This is where I first met John and Peggy who also lived on the estate at the time. They were passing by themselves on the way to the pub. They stopped to say hello (I think they must have felt sorry for me) and chat for a while, we quickly became friends even though I must have been nine, they were well into their thirties but trustworthy and I felt safe with them. I didn't own a coat up until I was sixteen (when I bought my own probably) and I was certainly never given a key. Without a key or coat, I visited them many times. Peggy was anorexic and John was working for the council and unable to read or write. I was devastated when I learned years later that Peggy had died as a result of having anorexia. John must have been distraught, it was evident that he loved her very much and she was his world. What became of him I don't know. They never had any children so, maybe, I was like a sort of a daughter to them.

I was often taken to the pub after this and *let in*, so maybe something had been said. So, at least, I was warm and dry. If not bored silly out of my head. Is this really what my mum did for fun? I often used to ask myself. Well, at least, it was warm and I wasn't outside in the cold in December without a coat. I don't know if, at that time, it was legal for my age or not and neither did I care, I was warm. So I would spend long periods staying with my mum in different pubs and many times I fell asleep, I was tired and bored with it all, I didn't enjoy it at all. Many people commented on a child being asleep in the pub and that it just wasn't right. I eventually stopped going with her and was allowed to stay at home by myself. As I got older I would occasionally go, especially if my brother went. I always knew I was safe with him, that he would protect me, even from my mum if needed, which sometimes it was. He always did and never let me down. While I was growing up, he was always my protector taking the role more of a parent than of a brother so I looked up to him as a father figure. At times I made a big joke of it and called him my father in front of strangers, which I found hilarious as he's only ten years older than me, embarrassing him largely but to us, it was a joke and we both saw the funny side of it all, even then.

Karl

We were on holiday in Ireland visiting our relatives. My Aunt a few years previously had given birth to a boy and I was meeting him for the first time, except I wasn't. As soon as I saw him, I recognised him as Karl from a previous lifetime, but his name wasn't Karl this time around. As soon as I saw him. I said out loud "Oh there's Karl" I couldn't help myself I was overjoyed to see him again. All of my family heard me but just couldn't accept what I had said out loud and so chose to ignore it. As soon as I recognised him, my guides very suddenly and unexpectedly stepped in very quickly and stopped my "clairvoyant" sight from seeing who he was in a previous time and how he was connected to me.

Perhaps it was to protect me? I feel it may well have been. I could never pinpoint how I knew him or in which lifetime and no other memories have ever come to my recollection but I did recognise him from a previous lifetime and knew I had known him very well indeed. He never seemed to remember me and I never told him my knowledge but still feel a deep connection to him, even to the present day as I am writing this. He still lives in Ireland, I guess I may never know how I knew him before. He didn't seem to recognise me, though, and showed no signs of having known me before so it appeared wise to me not to say anything to him, or any of the adults, for fear they would just laugh and dismiss it in disbelief, even though they had heard me.

It seemed to me at the time, that it was just another spiritual experience of mine, that I could not share (or should not share) but kept locked away to myself for many years, unspoken to anyone but known only to myself and my guides.

I'm starting to really understand why I was always told (much of the time) by the spiritual dimensions not to speak about the things I saw and my spiritual experiences, about my sight and clairvoyant vision though at the time I didn't realise that's what it was. I thought it was quite normal and that everyone had the same clairvoyant sight and abilities. Had I spoken about the truth of what I was seeing….well I'm sure, looking back, I would have been locked up, so it seems yet again that my guides and The Pleiadians stepped in and saved me. I read a harrowing book a few years ago of a psychic woman, who as a child had similar visions and was locked away in an institute for the mentally ill for *most of* her life. That's such a tragic thing to have happened to her as she would have been a wonderful medium otherwise. I'm sure these things still happen today but I *hope* that as we evolve that they are becoming less and less.

There was a friend I once knew who also had been abused and because of that was very *open* and sensitive to energy. She had a dark experience and was totally unable, unprepared and inexperienced enough to cope with it and the ambulance was called to take her away. It seems to me to be the case that so many, too many of us that are abused or experience trauma, then go onto the spiritual path. I feel it's a doorway (albeit a tragic one) to the spiritual worlds/path.

I also read a book called "Spiritual Emergence" but I forget the author's name. It was also of unbelievable things that nevertheless were happening and, had she not known how to deal with them she too would have been locked away.

Chapter 2

Age Eight

The Man in White

I was at my primary school in the East End of London, one that I don't want to name and don't feel any need to. It was after school and everybody had left the grounds so it was just me and my spirit friends and guides that I was playing with. Suddenly a voice in my ear told me to turn around and look up at the top of the stairs that led to the entrance of the building, which of course I did, only to be astonished at seeing a man standing at the top looking down at me and smiling, the *most beautiful smile* I had ever seen. At first, I was shocked to see him but once I had established that he was no threat to me, I felt okay in his presence. As there was no one else around I was surprised at his presence. He just seemed to be radiating white light, that glowed strongly. A beautiful aura surrounded him. That is the only way I can really describe it. He seemed to be radiating white light. He was a beautiful man in a suit. I will never forget him and, at first, I thought he was in spirit and not physical form. Even to this day, I am not sure and once you have read the following you will understand why. But he did seem very real and different from other spirits that I saw at this age. Although, if he wasn't a spirit person, he had one of the most beautiful auras, I had ever seen on a human being.

The words he spoke to me were "Hello" and that was it, I seemed to be under some kind of magnificent spell by him. He just looked so beautiful and emanating white light towards me. It definitely was a wonderfully bizarre experience. I don't know how long I stood there spellbound, gazing at him and his clothes. He wore the most beautiful suit I had seen anyone wear at that age in the East End of London, it seemed more suited to being in the movies. Suddenly, the spell was broken and I looked away from him and started running towards home.

Some months later, we were on holiday, my mum, her boyfriend and me, touring Spain and France. In total, we were gone about six months and I came back the colour of coffee beans. I loved it and we were in Paris, very poor and sleeping in the train station. The thing I remember most about that time was in the mornings when we would go to the same café. Well, we didn't have far to go from the station to the café as it was inside the station. The coffee and croissants ummm were so delicious. I was so hungry most of the time and was very underweight with long curly dark brown hair and a well-tanned skin, I looked like a street kid. The man who worked or owned the café used to give me free coffee and croissants which tasted like heaven, freshly baked and warm with a buttery taste and you could smell the coffee for miles away and the croissants just melted in my mouth. This is one of my better memories at that age.

So we were in France somewhere at an outdoor market, I was holding my mum's hand as we were shopping. Do you know who I saw? The same man I saw on the steps of my school. Now, you could say I was mistaken and it was someone who looked like him, but it wasn't. No, it was the exact same man that I saw that day in the market in France as the one I saw at my school in London, which made me think that he was probably a spirit person. However, I still had doubts. He had the same effect on me as before and he had the same presence, even wearing similar clothes. Now, normally, I wouldn't have said anything to my mum, I would have just accepted it. But this was different so I told her "Mum, that's the same man I saw at my school". Do you know what she did? Actually, it's what she didn't do that's more surprising to me. She never said, "Carol don't be silly how could you see the same man at the school in London and then in France?" No, Instead, she reacted very quickly. She grabbed me up into her arms and started walking very fast in any direction, it seemed to me. She never once stopped to look at him, or ask questions but was moving very quickly, almost running to get away.

I never asked her questions about this until recently, last year actually, when she said she didn't remember it at all.

That was one of my fondest memories of being in Paris and sleeping in the train station and waking up to coffee and croissants. I made a promise to myself someday to go back to that café, if it is still there, or any café will do and sit outside and have coffee and croissants, only this time, I will do it in the warmth of the sunshine.

The Spirit Money

I spent much of my childhood by myself with my spirit friends and guides. My memory is starting to return more and more of the connection during those years of and with the Pleiadians. I now realise that important memories will unfold, even as I'm sitting here writing today. And if it hadn't been for the abuse, I would remember more but my own mind is protecting itself from remembering. I also know that The Pleiadians themselves have been a very active part of my very childhood years, the lost years, that *I will regain and remember,* with the help and love of, and from them.

I was mostly out and about, often in nature (where I was safe) and which I still love with a passion. I went walking one day and found myself being guided by an older man in spirit to a block of flats nearby, where one of my friends Rosa lived with her family. I was in the stairwell talking to my spirit friend for a good hour or so. I recall that he was a lovely man with a beautiful friendly personality and an open heart who just wanted to make me smile and laugh, to make me full of joy and the wonder of life. I was only nine (I guess) and had not met him before or since. I'm not even sure of who he was, except that he was in the spirit world, but he didn't seem to be connected to me in any way that I could make out. I think he was more connected to the land that lay beneath the flats and had lived there centuries ago. His clothes fitted a completely long lost time. He was happily talking away to me for ages and I him, telling me that he had been there a long time, he just didn't know how long. But he had been there, stuck in that energy for a long, long time, why I don't know. Maybe he didn't realise that he was dead, but then he seemed to be "there" too long to not have realised that. Much of our conversation I can't recall but I remember I began to tell him about my mum and our lack of money, to which he pulled out some money and gave it to me. I was really amazed! I had never seen coins like that before. It was very old, silver I think and much larger than any coins I had *ever* seen up to then. He gave me the money and bade me farewell. I was sad to see him go, he really was a funny man and for a while really made me laugh out loud and lifted my burden very much with his happy temperament. The old coins were very real and safely in my pocket. I was on my way home to my mum. While talking to my spirit guides, I could hear them talking amongst themselves saying that I mustn't be allowed to show the coins to my mum (straight where I was heading) or spend them in the local shops. I was licking my lips at the thought of sweets, when, suddenly, I was pushed to the ground by an invisible force. I was shocked and stunned momentarily. The coins tumbled from my pocket and fell on to the ground and I was desperately scrambling around to pick them up. A woman who was passing saw my desperation and began to help me pick them up. Only when I was picking them up, did I see that they were different. They were not the same coins I'd been given. They no longer resembled the coins I'd been given. They were modern and new twenty pence coins and fifty's and there were only three or four of them. Gone were the old coins I'd been given. Looking back, obviously, my spirit guides had realised the seriousness of my having the coins and the questions that would have come perhaps even an interrogation, questions that I could not answer. I would not have been able to rationally explain how I got the coins. Many questions would have been asked and the answers would surely have caused raised eyebrows and bated breath and a huge disbelief. Hence, it was not allowed to happen as it would have caused too much of a ripple effect.

Slot Machines

Another time that I also recall involved money and the spirit world. We were in a pub, yet again and all too frequently for me. I was probably about ten, as I remember my Granddad had also passed away at this time. I often had many experiences, where I was told important information and this was one of them. I heard a voice in my ear telling me to go and play the fruit machine and that I would win a lot of money.

Well, it took me ages, about 20 minutes to get my mum to give me some small change so that I could go and do it. Eventually, I managed it, I don't know which I was more excited about the winnings, or the clairaudience that I had someone with me telling me about the winnings. I just knew that if I went and played the machines, I would win. While I was playing, I could see a female spirit with me. My Gran's mum, Beatrice, was playing the machine with me from the world of spirit. What fun we were both having, she was just as excited as I was. She was elated to be there and playing the machine, all the while laughing. She was standing in front of me on the right-hand side, playing and having fun at pulling the handle down. I now remember her well. She was using her energy from the world of spirit to control the machine and the outcome. The machine all matched up to a line of 3 fruits and started to make a loud noise with lots of whirring and music sounding "woo woo woo" very loudly. Fifty pence coins started to gush out. Everyone stopped to look, I mean the whole pub stopped, to look at this young kid winning. There were lots of cheers and laughter, with my mum grabbing a pot from somewhere and rushing over to help. The money was gushing out so fast, she quickly placed the pot to catch the money. It was coming out so fast it was gushing over the side and would have spilled on to the floor, but for the pot. We were all happy for a good few weeks, it was only fifty pounds but, when you were that poor, it felt like a fortune and it made a difference to us. My Great Gran disappeared in all the confusion and noise. I did not see her again for many years afterwards but I know she has often been there in the distance watching over for love never, ever dies. It doesn't matter, if you're in the spirit world or not. The dead do come back to us. I often felt her around me again, while doing some family research (2011-2012). I knew it was her, she had come to help me with it, I could feel her and hear her next to me giving me names of people and filling in some of the gaps in the family history for me. She was watching over me again. I knew how hard her life had been, I could feel it, sense it, smell it, taste it. She had missed her husband terribly, as he had died young and left her with many young children to feed and care for. Life in her day was much harder then with the daily chores of family life, raising children by yourself, laying food on the table etc. "You have machines today that do everything, we never had those, and even if we did, we couldn't afford them, they weren't for the likes of us, they were for the gentry", was what she said.

The Horse Races Third Time Lucky?

My mum loves horse races, so she decided to go one day and take me along with her. We really did have a lovely rare day out. Now, just before this, for a few weeks previously, I had started to tell her some of the things I was seeing in dreams and visions etc., things I saw psychically about people that she knew and would chit chat to when passing them by, I would see information about them, just little things sometimes and I told her this. I told her *some* of what I was seeing, so I don't know if she had planned to see what would happen consciously or if she was just being guided by her own guides and spirit helpers or perhaps a combination of both.

So there we were at the races. On a lovely warm Summer day with the sun shining and the clouds blue. I forget the name of the races we were at, though. It may have been New Cross. She was at the betting desk with me beside her, when I clearly heard the name of a horse being told to me, again by the spirit world. So I tugged on her arm, pulling her clothes and said "mum mum" quite a few times before I could get her to listen to me. When she did, I told her the name of the horse she should bet on. I didn't tell her how I knew, I just told her to bet on a certain horse, now, I can't remember the name of the horse. It did win, though, as I knew it would or rather as spirit knew it would. I don't know how much she won but she was over the moon, so happy, which made me happy to see her spirits light and carefree. She seemed to have a sense of freedom that day as well as if she was really happy and hadn't been in a long while. Poor soul. Not surprisingly, she took me back again a second time and the same thing happened, the horse won. She took me back a third time and we did the same thing again. The horse won. Now the same man at the desk where all this happened was the same guy all three times. He had witnessed exactly what had happened each time, with my tugging on her arm and telling her the name of each horse. He looked at my mum and then me oddly but nonetheless with a big smile aimed at me, while he was giving her all her winnings. Once may be thought of as a coincidence, even twice but a third time to get three consecutive winners in a row, with your small daughter tugging on your arm, telling you which horses to bet on is unusual. I don't know what he thought of it all. Yet, again, she never questioned me about this though or any of the psychic things that I told her. I was still unable to read at this time and it wasn't until my early twenties that my dyslexia was revealed to me. My mum knew I couldn't read and so knew I hadn't been able to read the names of any of the horses running that day. Yet still, she never asked me how I got the names. As for the names of the horse, whispered into my little right ear, I often wonder who it was that was telling me, was it my guides? Or some long distant relative who had passed over? Whoever it was on that day, it was definitely spirit and not my own intuition. I heard the voice very loud, clear and distinctive, which was one of the reasons I told my mum the names. Had it been my own intuition, I probably wouldn't have said anything about it at all. It was just too loud and clear. It made my day to see mum so happy that day and not having to worry about money, even if only for a short while.

I always wondered why she never took me to the races again, though. I think maybe it's because if she did she would have to accept me for all the psychic abilities, which would have had an effect on her own belief system. She would have had to change the way she thought about things and what she believed to be true. That is something I now know she was unwilling to do.

Chapter 3

Age Nine

Granddad's Spirit

My Granddad lay dying in the Sacred Heart hospital in the small town of Castlebar in the West Coast of Ireland. I still remember it as vividly, as if it were only yesterday. I had such a strong connection to him and have felt his presence close to me many times over the years (as well as my grand mum), I have smelt his tobacco which had a very distinctive smell, when there was no rational explanation for it and a sense of knowing that he was close by. He lay in the hospital bed slipping in and out of consciousness, sometimes not knowing if he was talking to me or my mum, as I looked so much like her in her own childhood days. He was very weak, thin, old and the life force was being sucked out of him. I knew he was dying, everyone did. I felt very close to him; he was surrounded by Angels and loved ones in the spirit world and I could see them. A bright white light seemed to glow and radiate from his very body. I knew he only had a week or so before he would pass over. He seemed to be half in this world and half in the other; I could sense this and he was telepathically talking to me from the other world. He told me he knew he was dying and seemed at peace with it. He told me he knew where he was going and although sad to be leaving his wife and family, at the same time, he was happy to be going. He told me not to worry. He passed away peacefully during his sleep that same week.

His funeral was a sad affair as is the norm. I remember it all very clearly. Hundreds of people turned out for his funeral on the day. My relatives and family were there, many of whom I didn't know. A week later we were back in England. My mum was feeling very sad and at a loss. I had a different perspective on life, on death even at that age. I was what…nine years old. He came to visit me one night a week or two after we had arrived back in the UK. I had just got into bed, feeling very sorry for my mum. He just appeared right in front of my eyes very clearly, very solid and real, I could have reached out and touched him, I'm sure I would have felt solid skin, he was just so very real. I found it a great comfort, I had no fear and was glad he chose to visit me. At first, he didn't speak. He just very quietly sat on the edge of my bed, smiling and looking at me. He was surrounded by white light. He eventually and slowly began to speak to me, he told me he had a message for me to give to my mum. For some reason, it was easier for him to contact me, rather than my mum directly, perhaps because I was only a young child and not conditioned to believe he no longer existed but was on a different realm. I do not remember the message he gave me but I know it was to try and give some comfort to my mum. I told her the next day that I had seen him, that he had come to me while I lay in bed. I relayed the message to her. She was very quiet and thoughtful, not saying anything, just listening very carefully. She seemed to be frozen to the spot, not moving and not saying anything, and her face just looked completely white, drained of all colour. I do remember that part of his message was specifically for her and contained information that she needed, but exactly what I can't remember, as it was so long ago. I don't think she knew what to make of it, or of me or the message. To this very day, we have never spoken of it any further. I do know that she had told my brother as he and I have since talked about it.

The Storm at Gainsborough

What an awful school that was, it certainly wasn't a place to get well educated at least that was my experience. The teachers were mostly bullies themselves and the kids were certainly learning well from the teachers. I remember one teacher in particular who used to bully me constantly. He was a horrible guy and an even worse teacher I would be shocked if today he was still teaching. PE was always a nightmare for me as he taught it.

He used to gather us all up in a large group and take us over the bridge to the park. Once there, he would call everyone's name and put them in teams. He always waited until everyone had been called, then look over at me and start laughing, he would then call out my name and start laughing in a mocking way and loudly order me to pick up the fallen leaves from a distant tree, making sure I was separated and away from the other kids. I was made a laughing stock and never fitted into this school. No matter how hard I tried at my subjects, I could never get them right. Especially English and I couldn't read or write properly (or rather passably) until I was ten, which is somewhat a miracle, really, because in my early twenties I discovered I have dyslexia. So considering, all in all, I have done quite well though I still struggle with this. We now know that dyslexia is hereditary and my brother also has it. Being that as we are from different fathers (so I'm told), I can only hazard a guess that my mum's side carries the gene. The schools where I grew up were in a shocking state and I suspect very little has changed. Negativity was rife amongst the teachers and so the kids learnt that they couldn't achieve. They learn that they will never get anywhere in life and not to dare to dream, they are conditioned as with all school, except in the highest negativity. It is a very sad state of affairs and one that we could learn a lot from. The children are largely overlooked. The teachers in that school, as far as I could see, were only there for an income and were not overly concerned with the children's education or welfare. Of course, my experience of that school was negative so, therefore, I have a negative outlook, looking back. I'm sharing my experience as it really was. I was continuously bullied and had few friends. I struggled with my subjects, especially English. Whatever I did it seemed to annoy the English teacher. She just took an instant dislike to me.

The PE teacher was a complete hypocrite in my opinion. He often had his brother into the school. Who was well into religion (Sunday Catholics), and he came to play the piano and sing religious songs. Afterwards, he would talk somewhat about religion and how we should be behaving towards our fellow man. I disliked him, with good reason, and he should not have been allowed to be a teacher. On a positive note, he did help to teach me to question authority, so it seems there is a spiritual knowledge to be gained from anything and everything we experience. Perhaps, that is why we experience it in the first place, to learn, gain and grow spiritually from it. Otherwise, how can we learn and grow spiritually, if we have nothing to learn from? The worst experiences in our lives are the ones we learn the most from, however painful, difficult, awful. We have the choice to learn from them spiritually and often learn forgiveness. That is when we grow when we learn to forgive ourselves and others and let go of the past, however painful.

There is only one good memory I have of that school, it was a happy, peaceful and very contented, blissful even, as I was in an altered state during it, but I didn't know that at the time. It is only now I realise this. In Winter, our class had been gathered into the hall on the ground floor, the room with the piano in it. Huge windows lay on the right-hand side of the hall and dark mahogany wood covered the vast floor. The room was huge and mostly empty except for the piano and a few chairs in the corners. We normally had assembly here so it was always kept clear of furniture or chairs.

A huge storm was raging outside and I happily ran to the window to watch it. The sky was making loud crackling, thunder and lightning directly overhead. The colour of the sky was very vivid and crisp, it looked so beautiful to me. I sat silently on the big bay windows watching the most beautiful sky I had ever seen. Even then I loved thunder, lightning storms, and wild weather. The colours were almost out of this world, almost as if the Gods had blended with the sky and painted it in their own colours like artists. I had moments of peace, silence, of beauty and all-powerful nature on that big bay windowsill.

I could hear the male teacher teasing the kids who, at this time, were beyond crying because of the storm, thunder and lightning. They became hysterical when the teacher continued to tease and taunt them. I sensed that the teacher was becoming annoyed with himself for winding them up and causing their hysteria in the first place. He was also annoyed with them, but he was more annoyed with himself for having created it all in the first place. The kids got even more hysterical, when a big rat ran across the wide open space, across the whole length of the floor. The teacher suddenly tried to restore some quiet amongst the young group, at which point I turned my attention back to watching the storm beyond the window in a peaceful manner. That day was blissful to me. It was spent in silence with my loved ones in spirit and my guides, all watching the storm. When my guides draw close to me, they create a quiet sense of peace within me, as does spirit. When The Pleiadians connect with me, the feeling of peace is really magnified and that's what I felt that day.

Long after I left that school, I had nightmares about it. I had nightmares about much of my childhood, that would wake me, sweating, filled with terror and memories. I would wake as if the nightmare was real and happening all over again. I would wake up in a cold sweat, full of fear. They only stopped in my late teens/early twenties, thankfully.

My Pigeon Hair

I was an outcast in my school and so, naturally, I hated it. I hated the walk there, I would drag my heels *all the way* and run around after the pigeons and any other birds I could find along the way. My poor old mum, it was never any fun for her either. She had such a difficult time every morning so that she wouldn't be late for her job. She always worked really hard, often having two

or three different part-time jobs on the go at the
same time. So I have absolutely no idea why we
all lived in such horrible, cold, hungry poverty all
the while. I guess all her money always went on
alcohol. Poor thing, now I understand the horror
on her face when I began pouring bottles of the
stuff down the sink. How angry she was when I
did that! Today, of course, that memory just
makes me laugh out loud to myself and smile.

On one particular morning, I was playing *really*
hard with the pigeons, which meant that she
wouldn't be able to get hold of me and yank me
all the way to school. I wasn't always an Angel. I
must have scared the hell out of the birds and
soon had pigeon poop all over my hair. I'm even
convinced that they did it on purpose. I was
mortified and made it well known, but still, she
sent me looking like that, even though I begged
her not to. She did this partly to teach me a
lesson and, partly, because she didn't know what
else to do. She had to get to her job on time,
regardless of whatever happened, she was not
going to be late. The other kids loved it, it gave
them ammunition to tease, taunt me with. I was
always different as a child, the other kids (and
even the adults) sensed this and knew it. Neither
the kids or the adults liked difference. I often
spent many a day out, while playing, talking to my
guides, who often explained to me that "People

don't like difference and it causes them to react in strange and horrible ways", It was always their way to try and console me.

So the pigeon poop in my hair only added to this greatly and that is one I will never forget. It was an endless day of bullying for me. I guess it was also the beginning of my own withdrawal from the outside world. I have lived on this earth during this life now for thirty-eight years, and yet I haven't. I've spent more time in the spiritual world than I have in the physical earthly three-dimensional world. A series of childhood situations, sexual abuse, bullying, poverty, emotional pain, rape and a whole list of things all took me out of my body and into the spiritual dimensions, whether it was the Pleiadians, loved ones or my spirit guides. Perhaps I just simply couldn't stand all the pain of it all, it was just all too much; one of those things alone would have been enough for me. During my childhood, the spiritual dimensions were the only safe place for me to be, and so that is where I went. Of course, my body was still here but I wasn't, not fully, that is one of the reasons I had so many spiritual experiences.

I was only half in this world and half in the other and so very aware of everything that surrounded me in other dimensions, the trees, the birds, the elves, the fairies, the unicorns, the angels, the

Pleiadians, the blue skins, the ghosts, the shadows, the light beings, the nature spirits and my own much-beloved Granddad.

That Pigeon Hair day as I call it was just another day where I escaped into the spiritual dimensions but more than that because, on one hand, I am truly blessed to be so aware and to remember so much, the spiritual truths, esoteric knowledge, realms/dimensions. Then, on the other hand, because I find it so easy to slip into the spiritual realms, I find it very hard to stay in the physical world at times, even today especially times when I encounter problems in my own life. As a child, it's what I learnt to do to *Survive,* I learnt how to leave my body, especially during the sexual abuse. Wendy, whom I write of never came back fully, into her body. Today, when I encounter problems in my own life, I simply leave my body. It's what I know how to do, it's how I cope.

It's very much a double-edged sword and I am still learning how to balance the two worlds and how to step in and out of them at will, but I am doing it, in a more self-consciously aware state. So I walk between the two worlds, like a Shaman does. At this point in my life, I am about to turn another very huge chapter in my life and being a Shaman is very much part of that I believe and I honour it so preciously. It makes my voice sing strong and my eyes weep, it makes me howl with emotional release from all the pain inflicted on my young defenceless child body, on the waif and stray that I was. It makes me stand strong, tall, powerful, a creative force with both female and male aspects of my self. Above all, it brings me great peace. It is my calling "Shamans are not made, they are born".

The bullies that day will not remember or perhaps even care about the deep effect they had on me. Their cackling voices pushed me into the embracing arms of The Pleiadians and love. I was surrounded by kids in a semi-circle, about twenty in total. There was a wall behind me and my back touched it. The sound of their voices jeering, chanting, is the last memory I have of that situation, until a teacher came to save me, though that may not have been his intention, as it had never happened before. When he arrived, I re-entered my body once again. The saying "...words will never hurt me" is a complete lie.

Words and actions can harm us so traumatically. They can force us not to be here. They force us into other dimensions. It is well known that survivors and victims, of both trauma and childhood abuse, in particular, have trouble being "grounded". When we become "ungrounded" we are not fully present in our bodies, we are somewhere else, in-between. This depends on the soul's evolution, individually, how much it can handle and integrate the state of awareness. Some do not know where they "go", they just get "spacey". The higher the evolution of the individual soul's journey, the more it will remember and remember where it has "been". Most people are not aware of where they go; they are just in-between and ungrounded.

My brother last year told me that my family at one time thought I may have been autistic because I was so good at not being here in the physical world. I spoke very little until I was about nine, but even then I still spoke very little, which, of course, in later years caused a big blockage in my throat chakra, so much so that while I was at college, I would go to speak and nothing would come out, only air. I have since done a lot of work (not only on my throat chakra) on healing myself of the past. I don't have all the answers but I just have some. One of my biggest soul lessons is to be fully *Integrated, Grounded and Present* and yet still open to the higher dimensions, The Pleiadians and Star Nations. Just because I'm writing these words doesn't mean that my journey is complete. It actually feels as if it is only just beginning. A new chapter is about to begin, has begun and "feels" totally different to anything I have ever known before, except it's not. It's just that I'm becoming more and more and more fully integrated between the spiritual worlds and earth/physically reality, and "Grounding" in a way I have never done before.

That is true for me, individually, and is part of my own soul's lesson. But it's bigger than that, it is also part of the ascension process, humanity's own evolution. The spiritual worlds and earth/physical reality are blending and becoming one. Not only are they merging, they are evolving and stepping up into a new evolution of humanity. A new breed of humans is evolving and it is happening now, not in some time in the future. You only have to look around you to see the changes.

My hair always seemed to be an issue for me. Many times in my childhood, things happened around my hair or because of it. My mum was devastated when my hair was first cut. Unknown to her, my brother's girlfriend had decided to cut my hair in secrecy with the conspiracy and help of my sister and brother. My mum was devastated and honestly, so was I. I just didn't say it or show it. Mum kept a lock of my hair for many years afterwards, in a book to preserve it.

The Native Americans have a belief that much of our own power and knowledge is contained in our hair. I really believe this to be true. After having my hair cut very short in my early twenties, my power felt like it had gone. It really felt like I had given away something of myself, of my own power and I felt depleted, vulnerable, my power gone. Through my own experience, I believe the Native American belief in this. Samson and Delilah also tell how this is true and many of our old stories and fairy tales have truth in them.

I used to dread having my hair washed by my mum. The way she did it was painful, cruel and unloving. The sound of the water would terrify me and send me into a panic. With fear and dread, I would listen to the water running from the tap, the hot tap, no cold water would run for me, just the hot tap even though they lay next to each other, they couldn't have been further away. She would drag me into the bathroom, the hot water already running, waiting for me like a trap. She would stick my head under it, never, ever using the cold. It was always too hot for her hands. It burned her hands so she never touched it, boiling hot. But she would always shove my head underneath it, cruelly and carelessly. She knew what she was doing but still continued to do it every time. I just don't know why she did it. I don't know how she could not have been aware of the pain it caused me, especially as she never touched the water, as she knew how hot it was. Afterwards, my head was always red hot and sore for a good few hours.

Wendy

Summer holidays from school came and I was sent to Summer school, not too far away from where we lived; Great, I thought no more bullies for the whole Summer. I had a great time those Summer months. I met a girl called Wendy and we soon became good friends. She was not what you would call normal, though, and away with the fairies all of the time and very ungrounded but she was a lovely soul, so gentle, she really wouldn't have hurt a fly. We shared many similar things, similar abusive situations, we were both aware of the bigger picture and had esoteric knowledge, fairies, elves and all elementals, I got on really well with her. We were like two peas in a pod, cast from the same stone. It was sad that I only knew her for a short while during the Summer and I would have liked to have known her a lot longer. We had a strong bond and were able to communicate telepathically like twins joined at the hip. I often wonder what became of her, knowing that she didn't "fit" into the "normal world" of restricted, limited consciousness that is in place to keep us unaware.

On a sunny day, we were playing together by ourselves, both tuning into a higher energy source and having a great time most of the time. We spoke to each other without words, mind to mind telepathically. During this day, I asked my guides what was wrong with her, yet I knew part of her was completely normal. I knew she was well able to tune into the non-physical world of reality. The answer my guides gave both surprised and sadden me. I was told that she like me, had also been abused, much of it by her father. In order for her to cope with it in a positive way, she had chosen, on a higher level, her higher self-had chosen, for her mind to go elsewhere at the precise moments the abuse was actually happening. This is very common with abuse victims. She was able to block out the abuse and cope with it, by her mind going elsewhere, elsewhere being the spirit world and higher realms of consciousness, which is also how we both communicated telepathically. We were both half in the spirit world, a higher awareness. What had gone wrong, though, was that her mind didn't want to come back and be grounded into her physical body at the present moment, because then she would have had to deal with the cold, hard facts of the abuse. *She couldn't do that* it was just too hard for her, she was too much of a soft gentle soul. She couldn't cope. So, hence, she was away with the fairies. I had mixed emotions about all of this. I was deeply saddened that she had been abused by her father, but glad that she was able to deal with it in her own way, by her mind going elsewhere and blocking it all out. At a higher level, though, I really wished for her to come back into her body and be fully present and grounded. If she had done that, I also knew she wouldn't have been able to cope with the abuse at all. She really was caught between a rock and a hard place.

That is what my guides showed me, told me, I must have been about ten at the time. Without them, there is no way on this earthly plane that I, at that age, would have had any concept of the information they gave me.

I felt much empathy and sympathy for her because I too, at times, during my own abuse had done the same thing (which is very common) yet my guides showed me that I had been able to ground myself and bring myself back into the physical world and the present. She wasn't able to do so at that time. I often wonder what became of her and if she was *ever* able to ground herself. It's a great shame but I don't think she was, I think from then on she was labelled as having "learning difficulties", whatever that means. As for the abuse, it probably continued unknown, in silence.

Rocco

Eventually, I did make a few friends at that school. They were Rosa and her brother Tony from an Italian family that lived on our estate. Sylvia, her mum, was considerably younger than her husband Rocco. It turned out that they had an arranged marriage when she was much younger. So he was well into his forties/fifties, when I knew Rosa. One Saturday, I got up early, got myself dressed and off I went to see her. I hadn't told anyone I was going, so no one knew I had gone. I was very much a street kid and was never, ever given a key for where I lived. I was left to my own devices and came and went when I wanted. I had a lot of freedom to do so, much more than a loving mother should give. Maybe that is unfair of me, she just wasn't able to cope with her life and experiences very well and she certainly wasn't a responsible parent she often made stupid decisions.

No one knew where I was on that day, I think that was my downfall. I was so excited to have a free day off school, no bullies today, just freedom to laugh and have fun with my friends. Or so I thought. When I got there, her father, Rocco, answered the door. He explained they were all out and would I like to come inside and wait. I could feel something was wrong, with *all* of my senses, I felt it. I said "no" that I didn't want to go in and wait. He persuaded me, though, to go in and wait, I think, by offering me some home-made lemonade. It was the height of Summer and a very hot day so I went in, ignoring my own intuition. Well, I thought to myself he's just my friend's dad, what harm can he do? I entered their home and he very quickly closed the door behind me and backed me into the corner behind the door. I had no escape, I was a caught little mouse, stuck. I had nowhere to run or hide. He was too big and strong. There was no escape for me that day from the inevitable. He was laughing and joking in a sinister way. I had never seen him like that before. He was looking at me up and down and then he started to interfere with me, I asked him to stop, he didn't. All the while, he was laughing and joking saying I liked it "I liked it, didn't I?" The next thing, I knew he was on top of me in his kid's room, how we got there I cannot remember. I somehow managed to wriggle my young body from beneath him, how I'll never know as he was so much bigger and stronger. He was a short, fat, wide little man and I was only nine, a little waif of a thing. I ran as fast as I could and I didn't stop, I ran all the way home, not once looking back behind me or stopping for breath. Only when I reached the safety of my stairs on the fifth floor did I stop and rest. I didn't even bother waiting for the lift. I ran up the stairs. I rested on the stairs to gather my thoughts, I didn't tell anyone for fear they wouldn't believe me and I was right. I wonder where that thought of mine came from at that young age? Was it my intuition? Or was there something darker and sinister about my family's dynamics, dysfunction, that I had picked up on?

My mum took me to visit them two days later. I wouldn't turn my back on him all the time I was there, for fear he would try and touch me again. My mum noticed this and once we got home, on the stairs outside our flat, she asked me. She asked me questions about why I hadn't wanted to turn my back on him. I didn't want to tell her at first, I thought she wouldn't believe me, I was wrong. She did, then. I felt so relieved, a huge weight lifted, everything was going to be okay.

She would sort everything out for me. I was wrong, she asked me what I wanted to do? Hell, I didn't know, I was just a kid, she asked me if I wanted to go to the police and then spent ages explaining what would happen if I did. I thought carefully, analysing it all. It seemed the decision was in my hands. No, I didn't want that, the police poking and prodding me, asking me all kinds of questions, the interviews, the press, the court case. So it was left at that and we never spoke of it again, ever.

I wish to God that, at that moment, she had coped with it better. I wished she had taken me into her arms and said it was all going to be okay, that she would take care of everything for me. No, all I got was what do you want to do? I was nine years old, I was dumbstruck, part of me just couldn't believe the way she was just giving it all over to me. The decision was mine. No, was all I could manage to say, no, I didn't want to go to the police.

I dearly feel very sad for her that she just wasn't the kind of mum that I needed but she was all I had and I loved her. In the intervening years all that happened built up inside me. She has done some unforgivable things long since then. I have forgiven her as much as I possibly can but I cannot have a relationship with her these days. Too much has happened, although I try in my heart of hearts to forgive her, I still struggle at times. I must let go of the past but that is easier said than done.

I was very relieved she believed me, and, at first, she did. It was my sister who didn't, my sister and my brother's girlfriend at the time. I couldn't believe it. My own sister didn't believe me? My brother's girlfriend didn't believe me? Not only did they not believe me, but they tried very hard to convince the rest of the family that it wasn't true either. I don't think I have ever forgiven my sister for that, I hope someday I will. So things continued, more or less, as usual in a strange way.

Monday at school was awful, I felt sick to my stomach, I had to face Rocco's children, not only were they his kids but they had been my only two friends in the world up until then. I couldn't speak to them, I just felt nausea, when I looked at them. One look at Rosa and her face said it all. She knew what had happened to me and so did her brother Tony. They found it hard to look at me. We all did. A silence fell over all of us and we didn't speak, or couldn't, our faces said it all. They knew, Rosa had this sad pained look on her face and in her eyes. When she looked at me, her eyes started to well up with tears. It was then I knew that their own father was doing the same to them both, he may even have gone and done more, more than he did to me. God bless her, God bless them both.

I was mostly in shock for months afterwards, I was mostly numb inside. I was walking around like an empty shell. My sister has a lot to answer for about not believing me back then. Part of me hates her for it and I don't know if I will ever get over her reaction. Should I even try to? Am I right in hating her for it? Would it have changed anything? I believe so.

There were times afterwards that I saw them with and without my family there. I remember one time a few days afterwards I was told by my sister to go and have dinner at their house. I knew I wouldn't get fed at home so I went there in search of food. I got there and Silvia and Rocco were having a big fight. I arrived and they continued, I'd never seen her mum so angry. She was yelling all sorts of obscenities in Italian, waving her arms and pointing at me, at times crying, then she would get angry. I had cottoned on that they were arguing about me. I could tell by her reaction, anger and tears that she knew what I said to be the truth. At least, I had an ally.

A few weeks afterwards, a rumour circulated at the school about another young girl from our school, who had also been abused by Rocco. Her father had gone and kicked his door in and beaten him, severely. Again, I felt numb and sick but I was happy for her that at she had her families support and that they would help her get through it. We never saw the girl again. She moved out of her home and the school overnight. Rocco and his family stayed put. No more was done or said and I don't believe the police were contacted.

I met the girl some four or five years later at the ice rink I used to go too. I saw her and her mum. They did not recognise me and I didn't want them to, it would have been too painful for all of us. I spoke to her and her mum and spent some time with them I even walked them to their car. Her mum was very protective, overly so after what had happened. I think she partly blamed herself, for what had happened to her girl. I never saw them again after that. My heart still goes out to that girl today, I know what she went through because it happened to me too. I never even knew her name.

My sister and her friend (my brother's ex-girlfriend by this time) took me to see Rocco and his family years later. God alone knows why she did that? It was incredibly cruel and torturous for me. I had to go, I had no choice and she didn't seem to care either. We were going and that was that, I just had to deal with it. At his house I saw that Rosa had changed very much. She was what you would call high maintenance and I could see clearly why. Tony was very quiet and subdued. I could see clearly why both of them had turned out that way. Rocco, their biological father, had obviously been abusing both of them for many years. Rosa had long ago learned that the way to get men's love and attention was through her womanly ways. Tony was in a state of numbness or trying to be, trying to block it all out and not feel anything at all.

I never saw them again after that and neither did I want to. Why on earth my sister insisted on taking me there I will never know. Did she really have no emotional intelligence or common decency? It felt like she was trying to punish me, but I just don't know why?

Very recently, in fact, over the last couple of months (August 2010) Silvia has come to me from the world of spirit, so she has obviously passed away. She came back to me to say how truly sorry she is for what happened all those years ago. At first, I struggled with this but I have forgiven her. It is not she that needs to be forgiven. I hope Rocco never comes back to me from the world of spirit. I will tell him exactly where to go. He is one person I never want to see again, dead or alive.

Around the same time (August 2010) I re-connected with Rosa through Facebook. She has had some tough times and they show, very evidently, she told me a bit about her life and Tony's, how he is suffering "mental health problems" which need no explanation. The cause to me is very very obviously the result of his father's abuse. Poor Rosa is very overweight, with much pain in her eyes and on her face. The damage that fathers or parents can do to their own children is beyond my understanding, but at least I wasn't his child.

Psychically, I can see and "feel" where both of them are emotionally, as a result of all the abuse by their father Rocco. And, sadly, I don't "feel" them ever healing from this. Both Rosa and I know that there are other children that he must also have abused. I don't think the extent of how many children he abused, or what he did to them, will ever come to light and be truly known. Tony has serious blocks in his memory as a direct result of his father's abuse. For myself, I feel I am a million miles away, in lots of ways, not just the physical distance but emotionally and some scars do heal.

Angel Spirit Lights

One of my earliest memories is when I must have been about nine. I laugh about it now and about a lot of other things that happened. You see I, at the age of nine, used to see Spirit or Angel lights. Now, if you are laughing at the stupidity of this, then you are reading the wrong book so put it down. That is what I saw. No, I did not believe that, that's what I was seeing because at the time I didn't have a name for them or even call them spirit/angel lights. I knew what they were but not what they were called. What I did do was to tell my mum who promptly took me to the opticians and rightly so. However, I was told there was nothing wrong with my eyes and she was not to worry.

I will try and explain what I saw at that age and still see today. All you have to do is try and imagine it, as you are reading this. If you look at the stars and imagine they are very small, as small as a grain of sand, as small as a marble, as small as a coin, now imagine that they are different colours beautiful colours and transparent, now imagine they are dancing in the air and, while they are dancing, they are moving in harmony with one another. Now think of something that creates a peaceful feeling within you. Then multiply that by fifty. That is how I feel, when I see these lights. What is happening is that my own awareness has expanded and I am tuning into a higher energy, while at the same time, Spirits and Angels have lowered their energy frequency to make themselves known.

These spirit/angel lights do, in fact, exist and many people have seen them, some people know what they are, some don't, some tell other people and some don't. I did know that my mum was very worried about my eyesight because I was so young, so I stopped telling her. I could feel how worried she was about me, although I still question it today. Was she worried about my eyes or was she worried because I could see something that other people couldn't, or was she worried about what other people would say?

If your own children or children you know have seen these lights, it is your duty to get them to talk about it, to describe exactly what is happening, exactly what they are seeing, exactly when it is happening, in other words get the exact details!

You see there is something you have to know about my mum. She is an alcoholic, God Bless her and part of the reason she is an alcoholic (just like so many other people who have addictions) is partly and it is a *big* part is because she herself has mediumship abilities and is very fearful of her ability and the things she sees. I am not saying that all people with addictions are mediums but many are and some spend years trying to block out voices and visions with alcohol or drugs.

These lights would move in a *rhythmic* pattern, like sparks of embers dancing in the air, with dazzling brilliant vibrant colours, full of life, it seemed to me they were dancing colours of light, that is energy, spirits or angels, of the non physical but very real, they seemed to have a life of their own full of consciousness and thought. It felt as if I could hear their thoughts, which I could, as their thoughts came to me in the form of a transmission of information, much like telepathy. Thoughts can transfer from the spirit realms and non-physical worlds into our minds, which is what we call intuition. Thoughts, images, feelings, telepathy, a sense of knowing, visions etc., all are a form of intuition. The more I observed and witnessed these little sparks of light the stronger they became and the information became clearer.

The Sky Is Not the Limit

I was nine years old when I had my first dream of flying that I can recall. I was on the tops of the roofs of my estate, just skimming along the roofs and floating about a foot above them. I went all over the houses, buildings and my own school. I flew around that whole estate looking down at the buildings from above, with a sense of awe and amazement. I knew it was all real and amazingly lovely, I had no fear, I knew I was safe. This was not just a "normal" dream. I knew when I awoke that I had been there in spirit. I can recall this dream nearly thirty years later. This was one of my first "real dreams" as I call them. This is a very simple name but why make it difficult, that's what they are - real dreams.

Many of us, many people intentionally and often unwillingly alike all over the globe experience strange, weird and wonderful experiences during the dream state. It is a time when we are able to fully let go of any conditioning of our thought, so that our thoughts go where they go, we are part of our thoughts and so just simply follow them while asleep without question. It is much like being in the spirit world. We go where our thoughts go, we are part of our thoughts, they direct us. Thoughts are creative, we create where we are going both in the physical and in the dream state. There is no difference, except that in the physical, we are fully aware and conscious and conditioned. Our conditioning often stops us from moving forward spiritually and evolving.

In the dream state, we have no limits at all, we create where we go. There are no limits of time and space, time is something that is man made to record events. There is no such thing as time, which is why we are able to dream of future events. It is all happening in the here and now.

I realise now that this young dream was Astral Travel, though at the time I knew it was real. I just didn't know the term for it. There have been times when my dreams have seemed much more real to me than the physical third-dimensional world and I know this to be true. The spirit world or other dimensions are much like a dream. It is where our consciousness goes without the limits of the logical mind and we are free to fly and dream. It is the place where dreams are made and brought into the physical reality, quite literally. First, we have to "dream" something into being into the physical world. It is where dreams are made. It is a higher state of awareness much like meditation.

I once asked my Tibetan teacher about this, I simply asked him "My dreams seem more real than reality?" to which he very simply said "Yes." He understood and knew that I needed a simple answer "yes" or "no", which he gave me. His own state of awareness is much higher than mine (if you want to put it into hierarchical terms). He truly is a master and I do owe him much for he made me grow. That wasn't easy and is another story.

Chapter 4

Age Ten

Princess May

I had just started a new primary school because of constant bullying, I think my mum had just had enough of it and was worried for me. It was further than my previous one, which meant a bus journey of about thirty minutes. The new school was lovely and I liked everything about it. It was completely different from my old school. I made new friends and felt I could relate to the teachers on some level. I found them to be open, friendly and caring, not at all like my old school where no one gave a hoot, especially the teachers or so it seemed to me.

The school was the best I had been to and a sense of happiness washed over me, a feeling of being at peace in school. Somewhere, I could be myself and it was okay to do that, to a certain degree anyway. I have three main memories of this school. The first is about hunger, the second is about the school being haunted by ghosts. They were earthbound, stuck and unable to move on into the light. I was able to see them clearly and regularly spoke to them. The third is meeting my friend Marjorie.

A Plate Full of Water

We lived in this awful council block in the East
End of London. It was even blown up in the end
because it was so bad. We were very poor,
which was only made excessively worse by my
mum's alcohol addiction. I often wonder, though,
if we were really that poor or was our poverty
self-induced by her drinking? Did she have more
problems than we wanted to admit as a family? I
remember it all too well and clearly. The poverty
of it all, was it all because she just wasn't able to
cope with life, her experiences?

So there I was at my new school really enjoying
it, making new friends and being really happy
again. One particular day we were all having
lunch in the dining hall. The teachers used to
come in and have lunch with the kids. The kids
were all lining up to get lunch. I was so hungry I
was salivating, which wasn't funny at all. I had
got my lunch tray and as I was getting some
water I accidentally spilt half of the jug on to my
plate. I was devastated. It was the only meal I
was getting those days, if it was taken away I
wouldn't get to eat anything at all that day. The
whole lunch hall suddenly became very silent and

everyone was looking in my direction. I must
have made a noise like gasping or something. I
was this skinny nervous little kid. I was so scared
that either the dinner ladies or the teachers would
take away my food for being clumsy and not give
me anything else. It never occurred to me they
would simply replace it. I guess I was used to
going without. So I tried unsuccessfully to
pretend nothing had happened and that my food
wasn't swimming in water. I was so hungry I
went quickly to my seat before anyone could take
it away and sat down and started eating.
Everybody saw and no one said a word to me
about it, including my friends. I was so very
thankful they didn't.

I remember one teacher, in particular, her
thoughts just naturally came into my own mind.
Whilst she was watching me, as I looked up at
her, my eyes were pleading her to stay where
she was and not speak a word of it to anyone.
She saw more of me that day, perhaps more than
she wanted to. Her thoughts were very clearly
written all over her face. She knew what my
home situation was with regards to food. I was
so thankful that she didn't get up and speak to
me about it, but she knew. I knew intuitively at
the moment, she saw my situation clearly, as it
really was. No words were spoken but she knew.
For that reason (I guess) she just sat quietly and

sadly watching me.

Years later I once read a book by Virginia Andrews where she is describing in detail a scene of a young girl who had little food. I often felt the same way. She described that young girl, even now in restaurants or when out eating with friends, I wonder if I look at my food in a certain way, or eat in a certain way that reveals that I've known real hunger. Part of me used to want to try and hide the tell-tale signs (if they were there at all), now I'm not so sure if I'm bothered any more.

A Haunted Princess May

My life at the school was going well and I was making good grades. The school was very haunted as I remember, there were at least five spirit friends who spoke to me on a daily basis. I didn't find it scary at all, in fact, I found it quite comforting. Two of them appeared to me one day very clearly and started talking. They were both dressed in clothes similar to those worn by maids of the olden days gone by. I was on the stairs near the headmistress's room on my way to see her, when they appeared and stopped me.

They were quite surprised but happy I could see and talk to them.

Before this occurrence, there was a rumour going around the school that a young girl had fallen to her death but I didn't believe it. I thought it was just all nonsense, only to find out otherwise from the horse's mouth. She had indeed been pushed to her death, caused mostly by jealousy, I believe. She seemed to be earthbound and stuck unable to move into the light. I was constantly talking to these two girls. They must have been in their late teens or early twenties. After talking to them for some time, I realised I had to talk to the headmistress so I bade my farewells, for that day anyway. I opened the door which was very near where one of the young girls had tragically died. I entered to see the headmistress, her face was a ghostly white. She must have heard or seen me or both. She started to ask me questions like who was I talking to and what were their names? She seemed a bit scared but open and was willing to listen, while wanting to know more, all at the same time. So I told her, she was silent and watching me very closely. She did, however, believe me, but she seemed to be grappling with her own beliefs, as if she had just opened her eyes for the first time and didn't know what to make of it all, I could see her mulling all this over in her mind. She seemed to be going through her own realisation at the time, with everything I was telling her. It seemed to be very important to her. As if she was on the verge of being a believer, this must have been a big thing for her at the time, as she had recently lost her mum to the world of spirit a few months before. It was a blessing in disguise for her that day. It seemed to open her heart to being spiritual. I know that she had sensed the two young girls in spirit. They were directly outside her office. She probably heard them as well, maybe even talking and walking about. She knew I was speaking the truth and she wanted to discover more for herself. I later found out that she had started going to spiritualist churches, I think to try and contact her mum in spirit. I hope she was able to. I had a part to play that day in opening her own awareness, though I didn't realise it at the time. She is probably in the spirit world herself today, I'm sure she and her mum are together in peace.

Marjorie at Princess May

I met Marjorie at this school and we instantly become very good friends. We sat on the stairs the first day we met while I spoke to her of a time when we had known each other before. As I told her she began to remember a time when we were brothers in Africa, we were a very close-knit family, Marjorie and I had a special connection and bond, so much so we had agreed to meet up in this lifetime, as well, but only for a short time. Marjorie and I had a deep connection that was definitely telepathic, the kind that twins have with each other. We often knew when the other was ill. It has been many years since I have seen her and she has probably long forgotten me by now, being conditioned in the school system. I know, however, her soul will never, forget. Who knows our paths may pass yet again but I doubt it will be in this lifetime. A bond like that cannot be broken.

On the Bus

I once also shared a psychic experience with my mum, when I was about nine or ten. My mum and I were on a bus journey going back to our home in the East End after visiting relatives, which ones I do not remember. So there we were on the bus.

At this age, I was easily able to read people's auras, see things about them, illness or physical problems/conditions they had, information about them and their lives, see colours around them, and know that they were going to say before they had said it. That was normal for me but what was more unusual is that this experience was shared with someone else who experienced the same thing, my mum.

I saw a lady on the bus whom I took an instant disliking to. We were both standing very close to her. I felt very uneasy in her presence and couldn't wait to get off the bus, just to get away from her. She made me feel scared and fearful. I started to tune into her energy at the time. I knew instinctively that she was a very bad person and doing very bad things. I also saw exactly what kinds of things she was doing. One of my words to describe those things at that age was "ugly", which is what I told my mum at the time, I turned to my mum as we were getting off the bus and said Mum "That lady is so ugly inside". You know what my mum said in reply, "I know", and that was that, we never mentioned it again or spoke of it further. But we both seemed to naturally understand what had happened and seemed to be very close in that instant and moment of time. I remember the lady quite well today which is not unusual given the experience and circumstances. I remember her as a very bad person doing wicked things, whether it was out of stupidity or not I don't know. I was able to see some of the awful things she had been up to and was continuing to do, I could also see she would be getting her own Karma and reaping what she had sown and being in turmoil because of this. Had I been able to go back and chosen not to see this psychically, would I still have had the experience I ask myself?

I would rather not say what I saw her doing but it wasn't good or nice. In fact, I was more than a little scared of her.

Mum Are You Okay?

I was given a warning from spirit because it was to help my mum, to stop something awful from happening. I had a premonition in a dream, when I was about nine or ten, about my mum. I knew the dream was real. I was witnessing it from a third party point of view and was not involved directly with the events or situation. I wasn't able to intervene while in the "dream state". I was only allowed to be a silent witness. My mum was at home alone. A man was at the door trying to break into the house to steal something, anything. I could sense his desperation. He may have been using drugs, I was never sure but it was the kind of desperation that comes when you are a drug user or addict, when the only thing you care about is the drug and nothing else, when you are so far gone and hooked you care about nothing else, not even another human life and perhaps not even your own.

He had managed to break in somehow. I saw this young man and I knew who he was. I recognised him as someone my brother knew, not a friend exactly, but more of an acquaintance. He was in our home, in the hallway, making his way towards the lounge, where my mum was. I could feel the most urgent sense of panic and fear rising from my stomach throughout my whole being. I had a sheer dreadful fear and panic. I had to do something to intervene or something awful was about to happen. Being a dream, there was nothing I could do physically. I was only able to witness and watch the events act out like some terrible play. But this was my mum, my world, whom I loved very much. I couldn't stand to just watch and not be able to do anything. The sense of dread I felt in my whole being, especially my stomach was rising and rising. He was almost in the lounge. When he entered, he saw my mum. I don't know who was more frightened, him or my mum. He obviously didn't expect anyone to be there. But his need for the drug was very strong.

There was deadly silence for a few minutes, though it seemed much longer. Time seemed to have stopped still and everything was in slow motion, the kind of slow motion that many people experience when they witness an accident.

He didn't speak, my mum was the first to break the silence and asked: "what are you doing here?" He didn't reply and never said a word. In fact, I don't believe he ever said a word during the whole time he was in our home.

He had something in his hand that resembled an ice pick. I was frozen with fear, but it was only a dream, right? He lunged at my mum and landed on top of her on the floor. He drove this thing, the ice pick into her neck and within a matter of minutes, she was still and lifeless.

It all happened very quickly, from the time he broke into our home to the time he killed her. Only five maybe ten or minutes had passed, but it seemed much longer. I woke up, I knew it was a premonition, I knew that I was being shown the future, I just knew.

About two weeks later, I had an awful sense of dread that something terrible was going to happen. I remembered the dream and knew exactly what it was. It was going to happen that day, just the way it had in my premonition, unless I got my mum out of our home. It was lunchtime, I begged and begged her with everything I had to take me out. I didn't say why for fear she wouldn't believe me and call me silly and stay in. She eventually gave in to my pleas. We were outside on a lovely warm, sunny day and my awful feeling of dread was beginning to shift a little. We were heading towards the park, walking with my little hand in hers. I saw a man; he was alone, I was stunned into silence. It was him, the man in my dream. He was heading towards our home in the opposite direction to us. We slowly passed him. At that moment I knew it was okay. The moment had passed and my mum was safe outside. As long as we stayed away from our home for a good few hours, all would be well. She would not die on that day and her life was saved. When we got back home, our front door had been forced open. My mum was surprised. I was not.

I thank God and my spirit guides for showing me the future in that dream. I do not doubt that I was shown a glimpse of my mum's future, the reason being I was able to intervene and change it. I was young, innocent and unconditioned to the ways of the world. I never told my mum or anyone else about the premonition either. This premonition was awful at the time, my sense of panic was immense but I was truly grateful to have received it.

Many times over the years, I've experienced that feeling of dread, fear, and panic. It is so strong that it leaves me feeling physically sick and has a certain smell to it. The horrible feeling that I cannot even begin to try and explain can stay with me for a few weeks afterwards but this normally only happens in extreme tragic cases, like murder. At the age of seventeen, I woke up and went downstairs for breakfast. At the time I was living in Falmouth with my sister's dad and sister in his home. The telly was already on and tea was being made. When I caught the news of my "dream" having just witnessed it during my sleep time again I felt sick with nausea and that dreadful feeling. At the time, I was so very shocked and stunned. I just couldn't believe that my dream was on the news. I tried to look normal in front of my family, I don't know if they noticed my reaction or not, I tried to cover it up and I never told them. But I knew, I knew about details of the incident that the news wasn't saying about the murder of the two girls, and I kept *very quiet* about it. Since that first time, I have had many more of those dreams, and experiences.

Once, I had something so bad, that I just had to tell the police, which I did, and was able to help. Since then, I've been able to help the police on quite a few different occasions. But I don't like it, I don't like it at all, doing that kind of police work which makes me physically sick because, more often than not, I feel how the perpetrator feels and thinks. It leaves me feeling sick to my stomach. That is the feeling that I can't fully describe but other mediums who have also experienced this kind of work will know exactly what I mean. I guess we all have a part in us that, at times, knows everything and can at times become activated. Perhaps, it is a part of a greater consciousness that helps us to know that we are all connected. This sick feeling reflects the negative side of human nature. Good and bad are part of our experiences. It is, unfortunately, part of our evolution. The gift of mediumship has its challenges at times. The more aware one becomes, the greater the challenge can be.

My Sister Michelle

I dreamt of having another family and a sister, in a different time and place, (when I was seventeen/eighteen I met her again and recognised her from my dream). Looking back, I'm sure our souls were destined to meet not only in this life, but are entwined to meet up again in our many lifetimes to come.

We were sisters. We both looked similar, very much as we look in this life. Both of us have very long, curly hair. Both had slight thin figures and a deep love of nature. She is an artist today and has a son who is also gifted and special. Let me get back to the dream. We lived in a place that was wild and wonderfully natural, a place where nature was respected, loved and to be learnt from, a place that is very often in our History books. We lived in a Teepee, in Native America somewhere, a small community. We had many horses and other animals. We farmed the land and grew with it. We spent our days running through fields in the sunshine outside. We loved our family, our parents, our brothers and sisters and they loved us in return. Peace was ours and we lived in harmony with each other and the earth. We grew our crops according to the change in seasons and brought harm to nothing and no one.

My dream was of a sad day of unrest. The white men on horses came in droves. They came so quickly, unannounced, we had no warning. One minute there was peace. I was playing happily with my sister. The next there was chaos, as men on horseback were riding around wildly in all directions, shouting orders, burning everything, killing all those they saw.

Why? I don't know. I wasn't given a reason, perhaps there wasn't one?

They killed our parents and then us. They wiped out our whole tribe and burnt the whole area to the ground. Nothing was left, just an empty silence and the smell of burnt wood. I don't know what happened to our animals or crops. They may have burnt those as well, or taken them for their own use.

So I had met my sister before, we became very close friends for a long time, well into my thirties. Michelle never seemed to have any memory of knowing me in a previous life.

The thing about Michelle is when she was younger, she told me she seemed to remember a time of being a Native American and spent many of these childhood days playing in an imaginary Teepee, in her garden. I remember her and the love of our parents that we both shared. I know in my soul that I will meet her again in other lifetimes to come. I just know it and it fills me with love for her and the bond that we share together and with our parents in that lifetime, in Native America as a family.

I don't believe our families just happen haphazardly but rather that we have known them well in previous lifetimes and many different situations. The closer the bond, the closer the bond.

Many years ago I heard of a family or it may have even have been a whole village, on TV, who had all been regressed to a previous life, where they were all connected to each other as they were today, be it as neighbours, blood relations or spouses. It seems to be a pattern and the nature of things that we go back to what we know and who we know because we are drawn to them, this is not always the case, though, and there are exceptions to the rule, of course.

Sometime, during my early twenties, I decided to do a healing course, run by the NFSH. I felt very drawn to this course and especially by the teacher. I was very much looking forward to it. The teacher, Jan, I felt an instant connection to her and when I asked myself why I was shown images of that same past life with my sister, Michelle, and recognised Jan from that lifetime as being my mum. The older I get, the more people I recognise from past lives and the older I get, the more they also recognise me too.

It was also Jan who first told me I was an Indigo child, one of many. I had never heard of these before, of the term or the children. This opened a door for me, a very large door. I decided to find out more and researched the Indigos. While doing so, everything suddenly, instantly made more sense to me. I finally had a place in the world, where I fitted in, even though it was on the outskirts of society and "normality". It brought a sense of peace within me. It closed one door for me and opened up another, one where I belonged. There was a place for me in the world, but it was not constrained to "normal", constricted, boxed in society and its rules. It was definitely outside the box of normality.

The Indigos

Who are the Indigos? The Indigos are a group of
psychic children who started coming into the
earth plane, I would say. Sometime in the 1940's
when they began to be born and they hugely
affected the 1960's the time of freedom and free
love. They affected society all over the whole
planet hugely at the time. It was a big shift and
seemed instantaneous. They were the first
"wave" and continued right up until the 1980's,
though I have found that the dates are
ambiguous and vary and are not set in stone.
Then came the Crystal children and the Rainbow
children followed. The Pleiadians have since told
me and shown me that the
Indigos/Crystals/Rainbow are much more than
just psychic children with certain abilities and
awareness. These children came from "Star
Nations" and are not of this earth, and neither is
their awareness, consciousness. They are
cosmic beings who chose to come here to help in
the ascension process. They contracted in to
help save planet earth. They came from "Star
Nations" and belong to the family of light. They
are so much more than "psychic children"; they
are here to help us evolve during the ascension
process, and they don't "fit in". It was also at the

same time that these children started to come in, that children were being diagnosed with diseases, conditions, that we hadn't seen before, such as Asperger's, ADHD, etc. The doctors didn't know what to make of them. The darker forces at work, of course, knew who these children were, they labelled them and a new set of drugs was made and brought forward for them, to dumb them down. This helped the doctors somewhat to understand in their own minds, conditioned minds, who these children were, so that they could label them and help them in their own understanding and provide them with answers and drugs. Because the answers and drugs came from the darker forces initially, these children were/are still mislabelled, misdiagnosed, misunderstood, to be kept dumbed down, to be controlled and their light, awareness, knowledge, is to be squashed. And they almost succeeded. Almost.

Chapter 5

Age Eleven

Breakfast Anyone?

Most of my childhood was spent being hungry.
Some mornings, my mum would come home
from the night before and cook herself a lovely
breakfast bacon, eggs, beans, mushrooms, my
favourite, tea and toast. It all smelt so delicious.
I would stay in the kitchen watching her,
wondering and hoping she would offer me some,
she didn't, she never did. She only seemed to
cook for herself, rarely cooking for me, my only
food source was from school. My sister was
given the responsibility for feeding me but she
didn't take it too seriously either, only cooking for
me once or twice that I can remember. My
brother was out doing his own thing most of the
time. He came back home once with a huge
salmon that had fallen off the back of a lorry or so
he said. That salmon lasted us for months or so
it seemed at the time and was kept in the freezer.
Why we had a freezer I don't know because we
never had any food to put in it, apart from that
huge salmon. I'm not sure it was salmon come to
think of it but my mum did cook it.

My mum was actually great at baking sweet pies,
cherry, apple and various other fruits and

Christmas cake but this all stopped one year. I don't know what happened. I must have been about eight. She just stopped one day and went out to the pub, I never saw her baking after that. Her Christmas cake was the best ever and she would start it in October, it was well worth the wait.

One Christmas seemed more special to her for some reason. She had been invited to go out dancing so my sister and my brother's girlfriend were doing her make-up, hair and clothes and generally making a big fuss of her. It was lovely to see her so happy I was really excited for her. Looking back, there was obviously a man involved. Off she went out looking great, she went out for the evening two weeks before Christmas and didn't come back for three weeks. We had nothing no money, no food, nothing for three weeks during Christmas. Then a turn of events happened. The electric meter man turned up. We only got fifty pounds but God was my mum pissed off when she did eventually come back. Her face went white when she put fifty pence into the meter only to hear a big clunk, as it hit the empty bottom of the meter, she wasn't happy. She never explained where she had been or what she'd been doing or why she'd left us all with nothing. I was nine at Christmas. None of us had enough food and it was a crap Christmas, even worse than they normally were. I had missed her terribly (being only nine and still quite naive) but, of course, when she came back even then I realised that she had been with a man for those few weeks, she had gone on holiday leaving us all to fend for ourselves. It was a miserable time.

It was shortly after this that I took to stealing money from her purse, though I felt so terribly guilty I only did it twice. Money in hand, off I went to the local shops to buy some food, not just for me but for all of us. I bought a whole sack of potatoes and lots of different vegetables, milk, bread, eggs, cheese etc. Once I had got all the basics, I went in search of chocolates and sweets but it wasn't a priority, it was a treat. I had some difficulty in carrying it all home. I must have looked very funny at the time, when I reached the front door having heaved it all into the lift and out again. Here was this skinny, little kid heaving a potato sack and shopping that was bigger than me. They all realised what I had done. I made no bones about it. My mum was in hysterics screaming her head off in the lounge. We could all hear her from the front door, we all started laughing, well at least we all had food. The second time I was a bit more cunning and less obvious, I waited till she had gone out *before* I went shopping again. I ended up feeling so guilty that, I never did it again. The message hit home to her, not that it changed anything, but she was more observant about where she was leaving her purse.

A few months later, I was accused of stealing £100 only I hadn't taken it. She had hidden it in the airing cupboard in a parachute. Later, she found it again so I was let off the hook, thankfully.

Europe

Some years after this she had a Turkish boyfriend Hussein that she was seeing. He needed her help to get a visa for England. It was obvious that he was only using her for this reason. It was common knowledge that he had a wife and children in Turkey. All set out to impress him, she invited him around one night for dinner. He had complained to her that I wasn't getting enough food so she wanted to show him otherwise, I don't think he was fooled by any means. She called my name rather loudly so everyone could hear and brought out a plate of spaghetti. I was stunned she was feeding me?

112

Well, he could come more often if it meant getting fed. The only problem was she hadn't drained the spaghetti for long enough so when she handed it to me, it slid off the plate. I didn't know whether to laugh or cry. I just stood there gaping at her with an open mouth. Hussein said nothing, he just sat quietly watching and observing it all but he could tell it was a rare occurrence and he wasn't easily fooled. A short while after this, we took a very long holiday to Europe and spent months in France and Spain. We arrived at a swanky hotel, Hussein had just had a nice hot bath that he said he really needed to relax after the long journey. We went out to get some food and arriving back caught him sleeping in the nude whereupon, I froze. Was I caught again? My mind was racing. Was I going to be abused again? I had about five minutes before mum arrived after me. I stayed very silent not wanting to wake him in fear of what he might do, my eyes being unable to move, I felt sick. He stirred and Mum came in at the same time, I was safe. I looked at Mum looking at Hussein, annoyed with him for sleeping in the nude and exposing himself. She stayed silent but her face said it all, I'm sure she had words with him, about it afterwards.

We didn't have enough money though it seemed, and in Paris we ended up sleeping in the train station. I didn't mind it at all, I loved it, the adventure of it all. I wasn't in that God awful stinky flat back at home. Hundreds of people were all doing the same thing, so we were not alone. My mum only had a few pounds to buy breakfast and Hussein was some place else. We went to one of the cafes in the station. She bought me coffee, not having enough money for herself. I was quite used to reading people at this time and the café manager really was a lovely guy who had a heart of gold. He gave me free coffee and croissants for the remaining time we stayed there. They were so delicious, out of this world, so fresh and soft melting in my mouth and with fresh coffee a perfect combination. I could have gotten very spoilt, had we not been dirt poor. One day, I plan to go back to Paris and that café and sit with my coffee and croissant and remember the good old times, however few and far between they were! I know I will never see the man again, I certainly wouldn't recognise him, even if I did.

I think we were all on holiday to get Hussein a visa but why go to France or Spain is beyond me. Surely, it could have been done in the UK but there we were anyway and I was having a great time. It was while in Paris that I saw the same guy from my school in a beautiful suit. I told my mum. She picked me up and almost started running. I still do not know the name of this guide, maybe I will find out someday. I live in hope.

Barcelona was just as beautiful, if not more so. We went to see someone to help Hussein, someone important. He lived in a beautiful apartment nothing like we had. He even had a servant or two attending to his needs. Yet again, I was playing with the pigeons outside and got bird shit in my hair and I was distraught, I was crying about it. Since we were on the way to his apartment, I was kindly able to have a bath there. I stopped *playing* with the pigeons after that, I had learned my lesson.

When we arrived home some months later, I looked very healthy, we all did. I had long dark curly hair down to my waist, a dark bronze tan with big blue eyes that stood out even more than normal with the tan but also my face was very thin. I gave the appearance of being very healthy because of the tan. First impressions can lie but I was very happy on our extended holiday travels. I hadn't wanted to return home. I was never fully told why we had gone in the first place. I hope someday will learn the truth of it all. Was my mum just on the run because my father was looking for me? And had he found me? I know that one day I will find out but I doubt it will be through normal channels. I will be given the answers from spirit, when the time is right in my forties and have been told so.

Boiling Water

Mum would often come home drunk, often never knowing who she was bringing with her, which is one of the reasons why I was sexually abused so much as a child. As she was such a drunk, she didn't know what she was doing half the time, *at least, I hope she didn't know.* One afternoon/early evening she arrived home, I began complaining to her that I was hungry and she really didn't like it. She was boiling some water in a pan to make herself tea, which is how we did it, back then. The water was almost boiled. I walked into the kitchen and stood by the door. She angrily took the pan off the cooker, walked over to me, held it above my head and poured it all over me. At that exact, moment my brother walked in. His face said a thousand words. He started cursing her, to which she just walked out saying to me that, in future, that's what I would get if I *ever* spoke to her like that again. I was *extremely* lucky that the water wasn't scalding hot. I dread to think what would have happened to me, if it had been. My brother took care of me. He took me into the bath and spoke very gentle, kind words. My mother disappeared to her bedroom to sleep. This incident with the water happened twice, I'm sure it would have happened much more after that if my brother had not stepped in and confronted her about it. My brother and I were very close when I was younger and still are. For obvious reasons, I looked up to him as he as was my saviour of a sort. I'd always known that I'd shared at least one previous lifetime with him but I've since become aware that I've shared many lifetimes with him.

The Shivers

In the local pub, I sensed ghosts in my mind's eye and it was there that I first *ever* got the shivers which, of course, had nothing to do with feeling the cold. I didn't know what the cause of my shivers was then, but I do now. It's a change in energy. When spirit or guides draw close to us, they change the energy. It is this change in energy round and about me that causes my body to react in a physical way by shivering. This pub was very well haunted and the couple that ran it were well aware of it and I often heard them talking about it to the customers in general. I could feel, sense and see the spirits in my mind's eye. They were quite peaceful, just keeping an eye on the comings and goings of all the locals.

Drinking Times

Many times, I wanted the floor to open and swallow me whole. My mum did some very embarrassing things, said some horrid things and seemed to become somewhat stupid, once she'd had a few drinks in her. Not surprisingly, I developed a low sense of self-esteem quite early on in my childhood. I clearly remember feeling very low within myself. On some level, my mum had obviously picked up on this and decided to highlight it very unkindly and loudly to all and sundry. She suddenly turned to face me, I knew something horrible was going to come out of her mouth, so I waited and it did. "Get your hair cut, it looks bloody awful and really needs cutting". Those few words did so much damage and changed our relationship. From then on, I no longer saw her as a mum, but as an enemy. It changed our dynamics how we dealt with each other, how we saw each other. When she said those words she obviously saw me as the enemy and was treating me as such. My brother was silent. For the very first time in my life, he hadn't come to my rescue. My aunty did, it was she who stepped up to the mark and answered her back. My mum had made me feel absolutely terrible, I said nothing and stayed silent but I was distraught and my face showed it. I was angry with my mum. I had been asking, begging her for weeks to please give me some money so that I could get my hair cut. I had been telling her how awful I felt, yet she refused, only to spend it in the pub. Having said what she did, something had changed, our dynamics had changed in a second. I was now the enemy. I got up and walked out.

My mum has been an alcoholic from long before I was born and still is. If she were to stop now, I don't think her body would be able to cope with the strain, as she is into her seventies. On one occasion three of us went to a nightclub my mum, my aunty and me, little old me. I was only eleven, I had lost my mum and aunty. I was dancing away and wandering around, just looking and reading the people. I was having quite a good time. I met a guy who was older than me, not surprisingly, as I was well under the age to be there, as I looked a lot older he might not have known I was only eleven, and I should not have been there, as I was underage. We danced for a while, went and got a drink and sat down in a corner well away from the crowds. He had spiked my drink and I started to feel things I shouldn't have at such a young age but I desperately wanted to get laid. I didn't understand it at all. One of the bouncers came over and quietly with his body language made himself very well known. It occurred to me at that moment that the bouncer knew him and knew very well what he was up to, having done it many times before. I had realised at this point that he must have spiked my drink. I was all over him, which was very unusual for me given my age, and his being a stranger and all. I was lucky he asked my age. Suddenly, he changed at the drop of a hat, so I was very lucky. Looking back, who knows what might have happened? My drink had intentionally been spiked for obvious reasons. This was another close call for me and I've had many. By this time, I was well out of it and had trouble walking properly. The guy soon disappeared. I found my mum and aunt who had been looking for me and now were quite worried. My mum even went to give me a hug but then stopped herself.

I spent a lot of time in the pub as a child and met some very dodgy characters, my mum being oblivious much of the time and I had some very close calls with drugs and prostitution at a very early age. One incident shocks the hell out of me now but, at the time, I didn't have a clue of what was going on. We were all spending a lot of time with my aunty having a generally nice time socialising and having fun. Unknown to any of us, we had met a prostitute and her pimp at the pub. She was very kind and offered to take me upstairs to the bathroom to make me over. I thought it was great. I was at that age where I wanted to start wearing make-up. We were at my auntie's house, so off we went. We spent about an hour in the bathroom while her pimp was waiting. Obviously, it had been planned between them both. I heard lots of noise and arguing downstairs. From the gist of it, my family had cottoned on to what they had planned for me. I was very lucky and who knows where I may have ended up that day, if there hadn't been an intervention by my family. I was obviously being groomed and manipulated by her to work for him.

The Suits

The London I grew up in was like a war zone, a
ghetto and suits were not welcomed. I was on
the way to see my mum at work at the police
station, of all places. She worked as a cook.
There was a park nearby, where the alcoholics,
addicts and homeless people lived in their own
worlds. I was happy, without any reason, just
happily walking along in my own world. I gazed
up and saw an old man lying on the pavement,
just ahead of me. The closer I got, the colder I
became and the more I saw. Psychically my
"vision" was wide open, to the man lying on the
ground and his spirit form standing to the left,
looking at himself, in amazement, a sense of
wonderment, of freedom, of happiness. His spirit
form looked up at my approach, smiled at me and
then walked up over his own body into the light
that shone for both of us to see. I walked closer
still. A man in a suit on his mobile stepped over
him, his dead body. And I grew even colder but
for a completely different reason. I could not
believe what I was seeing. The man in the suit
was actually stepping over the dead man. I was
not surprised at all by the spirit man or witnessing
him going into the light. For me, that was normal.
But the man in the suit stepping over the man's

body shocked me very much. I still cannot believe that he did that, even in the east end of London, it seemed more suited to a war-torn zone, not something that you that you would see in a "civilised" society. The man on the phone seemed completely and totally unaware and unconcerned with the man beneath him, the dead man.

Our society is very far from being civilised. We are taught and conditioned that we live in a "civilised society" but nothing could be further from the truth, we don't. We live in a society where priests abuse young, innocent children and ruin their life, to name but only one thing. And then the church hides it. Our society is anything but "civilised".

As soon as I got to the police station, I told them about the dead man outside. They said they already knew and were just leaving on their way to him. I still associate this with "suits" and still have a dislike of them. Strange how the mind associates things together and leaves an imprint, like a nasty taste in the mouth.

Time Well Spent Waiting

At the age of eleven/twelve, my secondary school was set to begin and I went for a few weeks. All the abuse I had suffered as a child, had not been dealt with. As I was still living at home with my mum, I was still under her care and supervision. I decided to take matters into my own hands and do what little I could to escape the situation. I had heard at that time, if you didn't attend school, you could be taken away from your parents as a last resort. That was exactly what I wanted. So taking matters into my own hands, I decided not to attend school and I became a truant. I hardly went at all, probably only showing for three weeks of the year, in total. I would go the odd day every now and again and that was the way it was up until I was fifteen. Again, sadly for me, I had been overlooked by a system that was set up to protect me and those like me. Instead, I joined the local library that was less than five minutes away. I had been having psychic and paranormal experiences since I was born. I wanted to find out more, I was hungry for knowledge, just not the kind I knew I would have been taught in the school system.

I was constantly bullied at most of the schools I had attended, except for one primary school in Dalston. I was always an outsider looking in. I was mocked and made fun of by the other kids. No one liked me and they made it well known. Kids can be cruel, just as cruel as adults can. The teachers thought I was a pain in the butt and stupid. I was a nervous, shy and awkward kid who didn't say much. The not so funny thing is that I wanted someone, one of the teachers, anyone outside of my home situation to ask me what was going on at home, why I wasn't going to school. I was pleading inside and waiting but, alas, no one asked me in all the 4-5 years of my not attending secondary school. Such a simple question, with few words that's what I was waiting for. Why aren't you going to school? Six little words which never came so I rebelled and never went to school. For a long time I felt I had shot myself in the foot only to realise, about six-seven years ago, that if I had gone through the school system, I would not have developed the way I have spiritually, so again it has been a blessing in disguise for me.

I was experiencing and seeing an enormous amount of spiritual things when I did go to secondary school, things like auras, telepathy. I was getting information about kids and teachers through clairvoyance and clairaudience. My own guides were constantly talking to me, I knew what people were going to say before they said it, I was sensing and seeing illness in the body. Lots of stuff was going on and I was never scared by of any of it.

As I was saying, I decided to join the local library. Having decided not to go to secondary school, I still wanted my education and was hungry for knowledge of the spiritual kind. My out of body experience, when I was twelve, was a constant thought with me and I wanted to know more from a scientific point of view. However, I quickly developed a distaste for science and its stance against all the spiritual knowledge that *I knew to be true.* It wasn't until I was in my late twenties that I discovered Quantum Physics. Thankfully, my opinion changed. Here was a science that I could understand and relate to and, more to the point, it proved that my experiences were real and taught me more about them, from a scientific point of view. I only had to wait some twenty years!

At the library, I didn't like the scientific books, but I got all the books I could about everything and anything. Spiritual matters were definitely at the top of my list and I discounted anything in the fiction section. Over the next few years, I read constantly, book after book after book. I must have read every book in that library, being a local one it was quite small.

I spent the next 20 years, in fact, reading everything I could still, book after book. There was a wealth of knowledge I could escape into where no one could hurt me, neither an adult or child.

Well into my thirties, I continued to read book after book. It was only last year when I was 35 that I put my last book down. I said to myself that's it. I need to stop reading and start writing full time and that's what I've been doing ever since.

There was a girl at my secondary school who, as it turned out, was not much of a friend. One day, we went together to see a famous woman about teaching meditation. I was only twelve at the time but I was still very interested especially after my out of body experience. I wanted to know more and thought meditation would help me get through all the trauma I had experienced as a child. Since no one else was bothering, I just wanted to help myself. I knew what didn't kill me would make me stronger. So we went along to the meditation thing. It was amazing, I felt instantly at home with the whole meditation thing and the thought process about it. While we were there, I did observe that we were the youngest people there.

When I got home, I began to meditate at once and it has helped me enormously. I don't have the words to describe how much it has helped me. In my times of anguish, remembering all the abuse and trauma it seems to me it has been the only thing that has got me through. I have watched many people over the years, (some very close friends) who have been abused as children, I have watched them go mad and suffer mental health issues, as a direct result of their own abusive childhoods. We all bear the scars of trauma.

So roughly between the ages of twelve and fifteen I spent at home in my bedroom, my own little private safe haven, reading and meditating. My guides often drew close to me and spoke to me, helping me and guiding me. I was waiting for a time I would be able to leave and my guides were always there for me. I never thought it strange that I was only twelve and meditating though looking back now, I realise just how young I was to be mediating but then nothing about how I grew up was considered to be the "norm". My guides would tell me all kinds of things. They started by sharing knowledge with me about my own life and when I had a good enough grip on that, they shared knowledge about the bigger stuff, about spiritual laws and the way many different things work on a spiritual level. At times, they showed me some of my past lives, at others, things we are all capable of, like telepathy, Karma, the spirit world, universal energy and many other things. The spirit world often drew close to me, especially my granddad and great grandmum.

I was left to my own devices for those years, with no one asking me questions about why I wasn't at school, which is really what I was longing for. I've since learned through the Pleiadians that things were exactly the way they were meant to be for me within the school system. As memories began to re-emerge through reconnection with the Pleiadians. I am grateful for the time I spent away from school and all the conditioning that brings.

Forgotten Memories

I forced myself to go to school one day as my mum was being warned by the authorities. Therefore my mum was telling me to go to school and putting pressure on me to do so, maybe the only time she ever did. So I made myself go on the bus, all my way to school. I got to the school gates, I stood there looking up at "The Big Black Gates" for what seemed to me forever. I couldn't go in. I was in some kind of trance state and was being told not to go into the school. In fact, it actually felt like a force field had been put up around me to protect me. The Pleiadians knew that all my spiritual knowledge would be either lost, corrupted, changed, inhibited, challenged, called untrue, lies, dismissed. They knew that if I re-entered the school system, all would be lost, that the very thing that had saved me would be lost and that I would have been lost to a school system of control, dominance, conformity, inaccuracy (especially in science and history), both on a huge scale affecting not only me but the real true history and science as I've come to know, believe and trust in, none of which is taught in that school system. Hence, I was kept well away from the school system though I had thought it was my own doing. That wasn't true at all, I was kept well away by the Pleiadians. My love and support from The Pleiadians have always been there, I've since been shown that, even at my own birth, they were there with me.

This is another memory that came to the surface while doing my Shamanic course. I had forgotten that it was The Pleiadians who lovingly kept me safe and well away from the school system. They saved me from it so that our connection would not, could not be broken and it hasn't been, but I'm sure if I had gone into the school system I would never have "remembered" the Pleiadians, who do connect with many, many children.

Chapter 6

Age Twelve

My Step Father

I think the reason the abuse from my stepfather was the worst and the most difficult for me to deal with was he was a trusted man living in our home. It had become his home also, I had never really trusted my cousin but he was a lovable rogue. My stepfather was different, I was over the moon the day I learned my mum was to remarry. I was thrilled for her, as this is what she wanted, a man in her life and a loving relationship. Of course, he was a drinker also and after a drinking session at the pub and my mum safely asleep in her bed, he asked me if I'd like to go for a drive. I didn't think twice, as I loved going out in their new car. Off we went, my mum totally oblivious, as I was, of what was to come. Well, he took me for that drive and while we were in the car he sexually abused me. So here I was again in an all too familiar place at the hands of a man who wanted far too much from me. I never put up much of a fight. As yet again it just seemed inevitable. I felt like a trapped mouse in the headlights not knowing which way to run, frozen in fear at the moment of terror. I felt sick to my stomach. I couldn't control the outcome. When we got home, of course, he went to check on my mum, no doubt to make sure she was well asleep and out of the way. She was.

I had time to put a large wardrobe behind my door, I found the strength from somewhere - fear. So, when he couldn't get in, he became very angry and started calling me all kinds of terrible names. The days passed and what was I to do, my poor old mum was so happy to have found her knight in shining armour. So I just never told her. I didn't want to spoil her happiness. I think I also must have had an element of fear that she wouldn't believe me, or just ignore the abuse. So I was trapped and spent much of my time in my bedroom, either reading or meditating. The only space I could be alone in to breathe.

I took to locking my room from the inside with some old rope I'd found in the house. He was hugely annoyed at this, as it meant he couldn't get to me when he wanted to. His punishment was to lock me in my room whenever he went out, either with or without my mum. My mum just allowed this to happen and never questioned it at all. I was mostly trying to avoid him, so I hardly left my room, when he was there. When he wasn't, I was locked in anyway, so I couldn't, if I needed anything, like food or water, it was just too bad. Basic needs like using the toilet, well, I had to use whatever I had in my room, a glass or cup, anything I could find.

One day, my brother came around with my cousin. They were quite good friends at the time. My brother did not know that my cousin was also abusing me. They started knocking at the front door, I shouted and shouted until they heard me. They were both shocked and angry that he had locked me in, but they still left me there. When my sister found out from my brother, all hell broke loose and she went mad with my mum, asking her "what if a fire started, what the hell was I supposed to do?" He stopped doing it shortly after that.

My stepfather's mum and I were quite close, having gone to visit her often. I loved spending time with her as she was so nice, a lovely old lady. How was it she had a son like that? Several times she has come back to visit me from the world of spirit, once to say how sorry she was for what her son did to me. She used to have a little dog called Dougal, a smelly little thing with a very distinctive smell. I've never smelt anything like it before or since and it was not very pleasant. One way I have of recognising her from the world of spirit is by the smell of her dog.

One weekend, while at his mum's house, his ex-wife was coming to visit and was bringing his daughter with her. She was quite a nice girl, very quiet, though, and she didn't have much to say to her real father or anyone else. It was then my guides spoke to me explaining to me why she was so quiet and withdrawn, not wanting to be in his company. He had also abused her, I hadn't been the only one he had got to. It simply never occurred to me that he had done it to other children. So, through the words of my guides, I was able to understand I wasn't the first little girl to fall prey to his hands.

It wasn't until I was sixteen that I told my brother the truth of what had happened. He was shocked and angry but he never really said much as he was just taking it all in. I had told him about my stepfather and he just listened. A week later, Del was in the hospital an inch away from death. My mum wouldn't speak to me, she blamed me. She blamed me for my brother beating him up, did she blame me for the abuse? In her mind, she may well have. She didn't speak to me for at least six months afterwards, by which time I had moved far away from London. My brother had confronted him in the lift and told him he was going to beat the shit out of him if he didn't tell him the truth. Del was still denying he had done anything wrong. He started to hit him, badly. He confessed and my brother continued, beating him to within an inch of his life. I never went to see him in the hospital but I did feel guilty, guilty for the abuse and guilty for my brother's actions, guilty for my mum not speaking to me, I just felt guilty for all the bloody abuse over the years. I just felt guilty for everything. There was so much of it. Had I caused it? On the physical level of course not, no way. The hard part for you to understand is that I now know that it was all meant to be, spiritually speaking. Like I always say, the biggest lessons in life teach us the biggest things. I learned that this was my personal path of evolution and I'm very grateful for it, as it opened up the spiritual path for me.

History was to repeat itself in a funny odd sort of way. About a year later, I met up with my mum, I had brought my boyfriend to visit some of my family in London. I had told Mike about the abuse from Del so he beat the crap out of him. I never saw it coming. My mum was screaming in the lounge. I ran through to see what was happening. Mike was on top of Del beating the crap out of him. Mike never heard my pleas to stop, so I dragged him off. The sight of all the blood was sickening. I called the ambulance. Mike had gone crazy and said, if he reported him for GBH, he would come back for him. So, in the two-three minutes that the ambulance took to arrive, it was agreed amongst us that he had fallen down the stairs. The look the ambulance man and woman, especially the woman, gave me when I said he had fallen down the stairs. God, I just wanted to scream at them, to tell them, all the reasons why. They, too, also looked at me like it was my fault. Guilt can be a terrible, terrible, thing which can eat you up from the inside out. What is worse is when that guilt is not justified and has no God given right to be there.

Karma keeps knocking honey

My stepfather is in a wheelchair today, as he has lost both of his legs. I don't feel guilty any more. It's taken me many years of torment, healing, self-healing, hypnotherapy, self-emotional intelligence, self-analysis, therapy, counselling and a vast array of many different alternative therapies, to deal with the guilt, to heal the trauma. I had to spend years peeling away at my self, ripping apart and tearing down all the layers of years of abuse. During my whole childhood, I was abused but it has taken me more than twice as long, to deal with it? get over it? heal from it? accept it? learn from it? live with it? The words I'm looking for don't seem to exist.

In the end, Meditation has been the key to unlocking my wounds. A favourite saying I have is "Go within or go without".

More recently, Shamanism has helped me hugely to release, reveal, uncover, heal and face the deeper layers of the onion. It truly has opened my eyes to seeing more, experiencing more and remembering more of my childhood. The memories that I thought I had lost forever are returning to me slowly and steadily, and many of the Pleiadian memories are at long last returning to me.

Walking with Jesus

"Someday my child, you will rise early in the morning, and smile again, but just not today, not today."

Throughout my childhood life, it was very difficult for me, my young years were fraught and besieged with abuse of all kinds, sexual being the worst for me poverty and hunger, an alcoholic mother - a rather dysfunctional family altogether.

When I was twelve years old, I went through a very difficult time and what I mean by that is I had just been sexually abused by my stepfather a few days before, maybe even a week before. Today, I have forgiven him as much as I possibly can and do not wish him any harm. He is wheelchair-bound these days, so it seems he has his own Karma. And I absolutely believe that.

Now I was in a lot of pain emotionally as you can imagine not physical pain but emotional pain and I was crying inside. It felt like my soul was crying. "Your soul is a droplet of the ocean of who you are", and mine was crying inside, so my soul was crying and I was feeling this as emotional pain.

This is when I had my out of body experience and I met Jesus.

I was lying on my bed crying, not just crying. I mean I was sobbing from the very depths of my soul. I was in a lot of emotional pain and I really felt at that point that I had enough of life. I didn't want to live any more. It was not only being abused by my stepfather that brought about my feeling. You see I was abused previously by other men. My mum was and still is an alcoholic

140

and because of this wasn't very nice when drunk, which was most of the time. I had experienced poverty, hunger and abuse. Now, this is in the East End of London in the eighties not in some remote African village. I was very underweight, I was skin and bone until the age of thirteen, I think it must have been.

So there I was and when I say I had had enough, I really mean it. I didn't want any more of this pain and hunger and neglect. I wanted to die and I don't mean that light-heartedly. I was thinking of ways I could end my young life. I went to lie on my bed. All I knew as I was sobbing from the very depths of my soul is that I didn't want to exist any more. I wanted out.

I lay down on my bed and fell asleep. The next thing I knew, I was in the corner of the room at ceiling height, looking down on myself. I don't know how long I was there, time ceased to exist while I was experiencing this. I went through a tunnel of the most amazing pure, brilliant white light but the funny thing is it didn't hurt my eyes. It was amazing! It was very loving and it completely surrounded me. I was surrounded by this everywhere and yet it seemed I was a part of it, all at the same time, which means it was a part of me, without my physical body or shell. It was me but without my physical body en-captured in this beautiful loving white light that was very pure, but it was also part of me all at the same time.

At the end of the tunnel, I could see Jesus and I moved towards him. He took me on a journey and showed me the biggest answer to my question. Why was I having such a horrible childhood and experiences? "Someday my child, you will rise early in the morning, and smile again, but just not today, not today." His answer to me was a complex one and much of it was received telepathically directly from him. He very lovingly told me that I was a spirit/soul in a body and that we exist, even without the physical body. It is the shell of our true selves, he showed me some of the biggest spiritual questions we have today about our energy and how it works, who we are, where we came from, why we are here, astral projection, the astral plane, that there is no such thing as time, that time doesn't exist, that everything we know to be true on the physical earth is like a dream and doesn't really exist. He showed me I would get through my childhood, that I would survive it but that it was also part of my Karma and that I needed to experience it all, that I had to grow spiritually. From our worst despairs, disasters, and experiences, we grow the most spiritually. "Only when you have crossed the river can you look back at where you have been."

He welcomed me into his arms and hugged me, something my mum was unable to do until I was in my thirties. I felt the most amazing feeling of being loved so completely. It made me feel whole and complete and filled me with love. I don't think I can fully explain this feeling unless you yourself have experienced an out of body experience. It really was the most amazing feeling of love, pure unconditional, divine love. He started to talk to me at first telepathically, then verbally he showed me many wonderful things, things to do with the bigger picture like Quantum Physics, the soul's reality, our physical reality of the world, mother nature, my own spiritual development and that of my immediate family, that all of my experiences however hard and painful were necessary for my own development. He showed me in the most loving and kindest of ways. It was as if he could feel my pain, which of course, he could because he is part of me. He showed me that we are all part of the same energy. It was when he had finished communicating the bigger stuff to me in a way that I would understand, that I was able to connect with my grandmother. Let me go back a bit. When he stopped talking to me, when I understood that it was okay, that I needed to experience my childhood the way I did, I was to further develop my consciousness to a higher level because of my childhood. When I understood that, he slowly let me go. By that I mean he started to step back. Our meeting was ending and he was leaving.

I could hear my grand mum in the next room, that's how it felt to me because I couldn't see her. All the while, I was still in the most amazing white light. I could hear her. At first, it was very faint, she was talking to other people about me. It then became stronger and clearer, as if she was moving towards me but I still couldn't see her. I could recognise all of the voices as if I knew them. As soon as I asked myself how it was that I knew them, that I knew instinctively that I had known them before, in a previous lifetime. That's how I recognised the sound of voices, I could recognise them but not quite put my finger on who they were. Instantly, as I asked myself how I knew them, I remembered. Before I had finished asking the question, I had the answer from Jesus as he was still there but not as close. He was drawing away from me and fading away into the distance and I was drawing closer and closer to her and could almost hear what they were saying, they were talking about me and my life at the present. I had not been able to enter the room where she was but was next door and we were all able to hear each other and communicate in this way. She was the main speaker, the others were just as important but further away as I had

144

not known them in this lifetime but a previous one. Therefore, I was closer to her in reality and emotionally.

They were talking to me verbally and telepathically, telling me that it was okay. It was just an experience and I would survive it on all levels, physically and emotionally. This was very deep and profound to me. What they were saying has been a big lesson in my life. The memory and experience of it has helped me through difficult times. I had to experience problems in my childhood for my own spiritual development. That I had to go back, that they all loved me very much, but it wasn't my time to go and it was now time for me to go back. Which seemed to be one of the reasons I could not enter the same room as them. If I had, they assured me I would have physically left this world and died.

While this was happening, I could feel myself being pulled away from them and going back down the tunnel of white light. Then I woke up, I didn't move, I lay very still and I didn't look at the time. It didn't seem to matter. I don't know how long I was gone and nor did I care. It seemed irrelevant, I just lay there with my eyes open in silence, taking it all in, reflecting and absorbing it, remembering it, I felt much lighter, both physically and emotionally. I knew that everything was as it was meant to be, that in truth there are no mistakes, everything is the way it is meant to be, that whatever happened to me however painful. I would be okay I would survive it, I would grow from it and it was all part of my karma, that I had to forgive others (and this is vital in moving forward and letting go of the past)

I knew I was going to be okay that I would survive and live to tell the tale of my childhood, however painful. That there were still many hurdles to jump but that I was on the right path and that whatever happened to me I would survive it and be okay. Even if that might take a while to achieve, it would all come good in the end.

All of the above information is also true on a wider scale for others, it is part of our cosmic truth. We are all one and the same we are all made up of energy, we are all connected to each other on a spiritual level, so whatever we do to each other has an effect on others. "You cannot drop a penny into the ocean without it causing an effect and ripple in all of the ocean, how seemingly small and minute the ripple, the effect will still be felt."

I have never told this to anyone before, not the full extent of my out of body experience but I have told friends aspects of it, in my late twenties. It was almost as if I knew not to tell anyone for fear of being disbelieved. Only now am I sharing it with you. I was not ill, I was not on medication or in a hospital or on an operating table.

I was in my bedroom and I was very much alone. I never questioned myself about this experience and I trusted it in the same way that I trust Jesus and God. Not until I was in my late twenties or early thirties did I start asking myself why did Jesus come to me?

I believe he showed himself to me because I desperately needed him to, that I am no different from others on a spiritual journey, that he came to help me as he would anyone. The fact that I was in such an immense amount of emotional pain at the time and was going to end my young life had much to do with it, Jesus came to me as he would to anyone of us. I am in no way special or unique but I am very blessed and my understanding of spiritual knowledge is much greater because of this experience. I defy anyone that would tell me it was all a trick of my complex mind/brain. I know in my heart, in my soul that it was real. There have been many true experiences recorded in one form or another of similar experiences happening to other people across the entire world and I am in no way special or unique.

I would also urge anyone who has had a similar experience, whether child or adult, to write it and get it published, get it out there, get it known, get it seen because you are not alone, or the only one.

Starman = Shaman

More recently in my connection (or rather my re-connection) with the Pleiadians, I have been shown/told that Shamans are Star-man, or light-beings (lightworkers) operating at a higher frequency. In the beginning, came the Gods, star-men who created Shamans, who at those times, operated in a clearer way, more directly with star-men. The connection between the two was much clearer, pure, more of a connection. I was shown in a very simple way without too many words.

Today, we have lost our cosmic connection (and memory) mostly but some are re-gaining and re-claiming it back, largely in their quest for answers of a spiritual nature, and their time, dedication, and life's work, soul purpose to the true spiritual laws that govern our universe. It is my belief that we came from the stars, were created by the "Gods" who were star-men created by source, otherwise known as God. We are not limited to this planet. We are cosmic universal beings, who are eternal.

Given my connection to the Pleiadians, that is still coming to light and unfolding more and more all the time. My story doesn't end with this book, but where I begin to share with you the information that has been channelled to me from The Pleiadians. What needs to come first, though, is my childhood story, as it was here that they first connected with me. But I feel the connection to them goes back even further than that, into a past life/lives. I am merely doing part of my soul's purpose but given my connection with The Pleiadians and my experience with Jesus at the age of twelve. I have recently been questioning if they are connected? Was Jesus a Pleiadian? Or from another star nation? I'm sure much has been written on this, though I've purposely stayed away from reading any such material, as I don't want any outside influence. I would like my answers directly from The Pleiadians themselves and they will come in time and be shared with you. It is my belief that Jesus was definitely a "Star-man". What my own question really is, "Which star nation did he come from?"

Meditation Begins

After my Out of Body Experience with Jesus, I woke up, I was so deeply peaceful, blissful that I lay there in a tranquil state probably for a good few hours. Everything had changed for me. Without that experience, I wouldn't be here today it had such a powerful effect on me but I knew that I shouldn't tell anyone, almost as if Jesus had told me not too. It changed everything for me, my whole outlook, so much so, that I began meditating at the age of twelve, alone in my room, for hours at a time. I would just sit on the floor, where my bed lay or rather my mattress lay. A mattress was all I had but it was also what I preferred and would have refused a bed if offered one. I would sit cross-legged and just meditate for hours. I'd consciously take myself off into a different state. It gave me peace in a cruel world. It was my only escape.

A girl I knew at my secondary school took me to a meditation event, in the centre of London. It was being held by a famous woman, though I didn't know that at the time. I still see pictures of her. Thousands of people were there, if not hundreds. She was a very famous and well-known woman though I can't recall her name. I often see pictures of her, still doing her meditations though and always smile to myself. The hall was huge. She had/has a big following and we all sat in chairs in rows. My friend and I were somewhere in the middle/centre of the hall. She seemed to notice me and spent a good few minutes in silence, looking directly into my eyes, I was nervous and felt like she was looking right into my soul. But I held her gaze, even while nervously giggling silently, as a twelve-year-old would. We seemed to be (and felt) the youngest of everyone in the hall. In silence, she looked into my eyes, I don't know what she saw, I was nervous, fidgeting and giggling but I held her gaze, she began to smile at me and I smiled back at her. I could feel the love from her, coming towards me. And then she looked away and began talking. It's only now I fully have some kind of understanding, how unusual that whole experience was, though I never saw her again. She still does her meditation event worldwide and while I often recognise her picture, I still cannot recall her name.

So after the Out of Body experience, I began a daily meditation practice, though, at the time, I didn't realise that's what it was called.

Chapter 7

Age Thirteen

My Cousin

My cousin had come over from Ireland to live and work in London. He was living with my aunt, not far away from us in the East End of London. I cannot remember who initiated it at first. It may have been me, but either way, I found myself in a relationship with him, which began when I was twelve. He was about ten years older or so than me. Today, I realise this was sexual abuse, but at the time I didn't, I really believed myself to be in a "relationship" with him and was a willing participant. I can only say in my defence that I was a young kid from a very dysfunctional family, who had suffered much abuse and was looking for someone to love me, in the only way I knew, through sex.

So there I was in a relationship with my cousin. I knew my sister and her friend (my brother's ex-girlfriend) had their suspicions about us, from the things they were saying around me and watching us both very closely at the time. My sister had also at this time read my diary, which did have intimate details in it, (as far as I can remember), though she never confronted me about it. I wonder why?

She may have been able to put a stop to it. My Aunt and Uncle also had their own suspicions about us too, as I often used to go over and spend the night with them, or rather my cousin, always pretending to sleep on their couch. One time, my uncle did question me about what bedding I was using but I just made up some story and he left it at that. I thought the world of my cousin at the time and believed myself to be in love with him, so who better to lose my virginity to? One night, I decided to have full sex with him, I lost my virginity to my cousin, while staying at my aunt's house. I thought I was all grown up then, little did I know I was still a little girl being sexually abused *yet again*. At the time, I didn't think he even realised I was a virgin. We had never spoken of it. It was a very strange "relationship" we had, but looking back, of course, he must have realised it, being older and wiser than me. Afterwards, there was blood on the sheets, I looked at him and for a few seconds and in his eyes I could see a look of disgust at himself, for what he had done, for what "we" had done. He was very quiet after that and we just lay there gazing at each other without words and we drifted off to sleep like that. Afterwards, we continued in a "relationship" for about six months to a year in total. At the time, I thought he was the bee's knees being older, wiser and a charmer.

He used to come and visit me secretly and no one confronted either of us, although people did have their suspicions, my sister, her friend, my aunt and uncle. I think my mum even had her own suspicions as to what was going on but no one said or did anything. Even after reading my diary, my sister never said or did anything and, when I look back on it all it all seems even more strange to me now than it did then.

One afternoon, he came around to see me, in secret, as normal. When he turned up, he was extremely drunk and could barely walk or stand up straight.

That was the day that he raped me when I was only just thirteen. I really don't believe that he meant to, I didn't believe it then and I still don't believe it now. He was drunk, who knew what was going on in his head really? But he still did it anyway. He fell asleep afterwards, on top of me, a dead weight in a drunken stupor. I managed to wriggle myself out from underneath him. Everything had changed. All of my feelings towards him were gone and changed. I didn't want to be anywhere near him any more.

I ran to the bathroom, poured myself a hot bath

and scrubbed myself until I was red and raw all over and very sore. But I still didn't feel clean, I felt dirty and unclean and, no matter how much I scrubbed myself red and sore, I couldn't remove that feeling, a feeling that would stay with me for a good fifteen years afterwards, a feeling of "needing" to be clean and scrubbing myself in hot baths or showers, as if I could somehow clean it all away, which of course, is impossible and illogical but that's how I felt. With that feeling, I'm not alone as it's a very common reaction to have and do. I never told anyone that I had been raped. I dealt with it by myself as best I could. Looking back, I think I must have been in shock for a good few months afterwards.

My period was late. I knew I was pregnant. *Emotionally, I was in turmoil and really didn't know what to do.* My stomach had grown and my brother noticed it. He even asked my mum (in front of me) "Was I pregnant?" to which she replied "No" and then was silent. The subject changed. And I said nothing, the fear growing within me of what I was to do? At thirteen and pregnant. I was a skinny thing and still undernourished from lack of food and with what seemed to me, a huge belly that showed. And it showed enough for my brother to ask the question. I was so very scared and time was going on, I had no one to confide in, or chose not to, as I always had my brother. I didn't know what to do. I was in a daze about it all. I spent many days alone in my room trying to figure it out myself. I was too young to have a child and *I certainly didn't want to have a child that had come about from being raped by my cousin at the age of thirteen.* I didn't want it and would do anything to get rid of it, even harm my self. I was in turmoil. Then the day came I knew what to do. Another very strange conversation I was overhearing. My sister and her friend were having the weirdest conversation right in front of me. And I still believe it was for me that they were having it. Why else? Although consciously I don't think they knew, I would like to think that they would have stepped in and cared enough to help. They were talking about young girls being pregnant and poking themselves with knitting needles in order to lose the baby. I was stunned into silence.

I knew it was dangerous but I was in desperate need to get rid of it. I knew this was what I was going to do. I chose a day, a few days later I ran yet another hot bath while searching out a couple of my mum's knitting needles. I went into the bathroom and held it under the boiling water. I got undressed and lay in the bath. In silence, I lay there for a few minutes scared of what I needed to do. I picked up the needle inserted it and starting to poke it around. It hurt, I stopped and started several times. I didn't know what I was doing.

I didn't want the baby, I was but a child myself and I was scared. Eventually, it hurt so much I stopped.

A week or so went by and, while I using the toilet having a pee, I knew something was wrong. A strong bright white light seemed to surround me, encompassing me with a strong feeling of love, but something was wrong. I seemed to go into an altered state of consciousness, that kept me safe, quiet, stillness and peace surrounded me, a strong feeling of love again. I was in two different worlds with my awareness that always brings to me, a strong feeling of peace and silence with it.

I still don't know to this day how long I was in that toilet. It could have been five minutes or three hours, time felt like it had ceased. That feeling is common in altered states of awareness. Something fell out of me as I was peeing. I looked down into the toilet and saw something, that I don't ever want to remember or describe. But I spent the longest time looking into the toilet at it. Suddenly, I seemed to snap out of it, the altered state of awareness. I flushed the toilet and that was that. I knew it was over. I felt numb, I went to lie down and spent weeks in my room, just what I wanted, just to be left alone. To this day, I still cannot be sure what caused my miscarriage. Was it just a natural occurrence that would have happened anyway? Or was I solely responsible? Either way, I felt responsible. Some things are best left unknown, they just drag up too much emotion with them. I just really didn't want to even think about it any more.

We had a neighbour who lived beneath us on the fourth floor. He was a nice, kind, gentleman and I liked him. I remember he always used to playfully tease me about my curly hair and call me "curly wurly" whenever I saw him. I met him in the lift one day shortly afterwards. Again it was another one of the strangest and unbelievable conversations, that I kept seeming to have and come across as a child. He began to tell me about a foetus that he had found in his own toilet recently. He was saying that he knew all about the pipes, how they worked and how the natural flow of them goes down. He went on to say that what he found must have come from our own flat or one of the flats above us. I froze and didn't say anything. I thought it was all behind me and forgotten. He just stared at me, I guess he realised at the moment due to my face and the look of personal horror on my face, that it was me. I went as white as a ghost. I started to feel sick, sick at what I'd done to an unborn foetus,

160

there was *no question* in my mind. The cold hard facts hit me. I got out of the lift in search of peace and solitude. I never saw him again but at least I was no longer pregnant.

I promised to myself that day, that as soon as I was sixteen, I would leave there and get as far away as I possibly could, which is exactly what I did. Some people say that our childhood years are the best years we ever have, not in my case. I was born and raised into what felt like a living nightmare for me. The only thing I *"ever had"* was my connection to the spirit world, that kept me sane and saved me from taking my own life at the age of twelve. On that day, I made a promise to myself. That when I was sixteen, I would leave that place and have a different life. I spent the next few years waiting and planning on how I wanted to live.

Earlier this year (2011) I had an experience on the Astral Plane, whilst asleep, I dreamt that both my cousin and stepfather came to visit me to say sorry for the things that they had done to me in my earlier childhood years. I know enough about the astral plane and the "dream state" to know that this experience was a real experience, a different reality just not the physical earthly one. I challenged them both during this, especially my

161

stepfather, who remains married to my mum, who knows very well what he did, but she has chosen her path and made her choice. And, yes, it was a choice, it was me or him. She chose him, one of the men who abused me. She remains married today (at the time of writing) and he is still wheelchair bound.

When I awoke in the morning, being fully aware of the "dream" and remembering it, processing the significance of it all, and the difference it would bring to me, peace came over me, a sense of release, a feeling of forgiveness, letting it all go, I felt lighter and freer. There was a feeling of forgiveness towards both my cousin and stepfather equally. I knew that they really meant it when they said sorry. They seemed to be speaking to me from their soul. I also realised how important it was that I forgave them. In forgiving them, I was helping their own individual soul's progress. Their souls had reached a stage of awareness, of what they had done and I had been shown during the dream state that, my forgiveness was "*for*" them and "*to*" them. Without it, I would be hindering their own soul's progression and also mine. It seemed their soul's progression had realised the enormity of it, what they had done and the negative effects, karma they themselves had created by their own acts. They had fully realised what they had done and the long-lasting damage, it left me with. And for that, both were equally sorry. I forgave them, in a peaceful way and I let it go, fully. I don't hold any resentment towards them. I simply forgave them. Peace is in me, I let go.

Another time was to come in the future when more forgiveness from me would be needed again, but I didn't know that during the time of the "dream" when I wrote the above. And it seems that forgiveness is like peeling onions "*slowly*" and each one is deeper than the last layer. I had thought that "dream" had been my own final layer but it wasn't. The death of my mum brought the final layer. I hope.

Chapter 8

Age Fourteen

Food

My mum became like a stranger to me and I had little contact with the rest of my family. I hardly saw them from week to week. I was quite happily reading and meditating in my room. I had very little food, though, and looking back it was *just enough* to sustain me. My mum wouldn't buy any food for days on end. I would hear her come in, go into the kitchen and put some food into the kitchen and then hear her leave again. I would quickly make my way into the kitchen to see what food if any she had brought. There was nothing, the cupboards were mostly bare, I went to the fridge – wow - I couldn't believe my luck, a huge cake from Tesco's! Oh, God, I was so hungry! I wolfed it down. I thought I was so lucky at the time to have that cake. This continuous cycle of having not enough food and then cake arriving carried on for a few months, until one day, my mum, my brother and I were all in the pub with some other relatives and she started to tell everyone very loudly how, as soon as she got home, I would eat all the food in the house. She was trying to embarrass me and it was working very well. What she chose not to say was the truth of what was going on, that the only food in the house *was* the cake. Was this her Intention?

Looking back, I do believe so, how could it not have been? It was a cruel thing to do, there was a cruelty in my mum, that raised its ugly head all too often, mostly when she drank and that seemed to be constantly.

Food was an unspoken big issue in our family for a very long time, 'The Elephant in the room'. It's only in looking back I can understand why and the full extent of it. My mum has an eating disorder. She hardly ever eats, whether this is because all she does is drink, or because all she does is drink and does not eat. I have to ask myself and wonder which came first for her, the eating disorder, or the drinking problem?

My brother was skin and bone well into his twenties until he moved out and started taking care of himself and eating properly. His girlfriend at the time was a very good cook and always made sure he ate well. He quickly started putting on weight and looking healthy and normal. He still has issues with food but he doesn't have an eating disorder. He has found that he cannot stomach even looking at fat on meat because of some of the meals that my mum made, for example, pig's trotters sticking out of the pan, with hair and skin still intact, God knows where she got them and the stink that came from them was enough to make us all sick. It is no wonder he cannot even *look at* fat these days.

My sister soon developed an eating disorder of her own, very young (without realising it) as she always had more body fat than the rest of us. I also had times when I've had my own demons to bear with food. It seems to be the case in my family that the eating disorder has for some reason skipped the male side. I do wonder is it because, as females, we have learnt the pattern from my mum, and this is how we unconsciously learned to deal with things. Would it have been different, if it had been my brother's dad with the eating disorder? Would it then have been my two older brother's who would have developed an eating disorder?

A few years ago, I was visiting my mum in Ireland, it was very sad to see her struggling to eat just a small bowl of soup, as her body was obviously starving and wasting away. God bless her and may Heaven help her.

My diet as a child was very poor and extremely lacking. I was skin and bone and how this wasn't recognised by my primary school teachers is beyond my understanding. I was starving and used to eat the scraps of leftovers. I used to have to do the dishes after dinner, so I would take the plates through to the kitchen and cram down the leftovers from the plates. I would always clear my plate and was always hungry afterwards, so I took to doing the dishes a lot.

I was taken to the doctor's on several occasions because I suffered terribly from constipation due to my diet or lack of food. I would spend hours on the toilet in pain unable to do anything. The doctor always advised my mum that the constipation was due to lack of fruit and vegetables and I should be put on a special diet or rather I should say a normal diet but I don't remember that *ever* happening. What I do remember is her taking me to Dalston Market, when they were closing and the awful stink of the market, mostly of rotting fruit in the height of Summer. That smell used to stick in the back of my throat, a smell of Dean Street market in Soho. Whenever I smell it I am immediately drawn back to my young days of poverty and an awful feeling of needing to escape quickly. It leaves me with an awful feeling of dread and longing all at the same time, a longing for an elusive childhood that I never had.

She used to take me there to gather the fruit from

the pavements that were discarded. Most of it was unfit to eat, I'm sure and I don't remember eating it, Is that a good thing or not? Nonetheless, there was my mum picking up fruit and getting me to do the same with people passing and staring, some openly, some sneaking looks, when they could. Pity is what I remember. I don't think she could have been in her right mind, while she did this, or perhaps she was and things really were that bad.

I remember the first day we went there, and the stench of rotting vegetables and fruit during the closing hours. Why it had that stink, I don't know but it did and it shouldn't have. Poverty in the East End of London in the Eighties was a living nightmare and it stank quite literally, boy did that stink cling to my clothes, the back of my throat, everything, even under my nails. Two or three times, my mum took me walking through the market, along the pavement, her head down just looking. I wondered to myself what she was doing when she *instructed* me to start picking up the fruit that lay at our feet. Not knowing what to do, I just stared and stared at her for what must have been too long for her liking, as she became angry, at that point. I quickly did as she instructed, without question for fear of bearing the brunt of her anger.

Chapter 9

Age Fifteen

Limbo

I had discovered another world, a spiritual world that saved me and I kept silent about it, I didn't tell a single soul, especially not my family. I knew that they wouldn't understand. It was many, many, years before I told anyone of my experience with Jesus while living on Holy Island in Scotland (a Buddhist retreat centre) that I first shared it with a friend in 2004. I'd kept silent all those years.

Here I was, aged fifteen, still meditating in my room and reading book upon book about spiritual and esoteric knowledge. I was in "Limbo", a space of being in-between, transformation, quiet solitude far from the madness. A separateness from my family existed, a void had grown within me, a distance between us. I knew I was different and there was no going back, no avoiding it. I tried to hide it in my quietness, as I still do sometimes. Nobody asked me questions about what I was doing, where I was, how I was spending my time. I was in "Limbo", knowing that it wouldn't be long until I was sixteen and could legally leave. So I waited and planned for my birthday. What I would I do and where I would go? I knew a change was coming and I couldn't wait! I was so eager for it. I simply waited for it in my silence, in my quietness, in my sense of knowing. I sat down and meditated and read with little interest in anything else at the time. I cocooned myself away from the world at the time.

The strange thing is, as I write this today, I feel I'm exactly in the same space emotionally. Limbo has engaged me again, a transformation has come again or, at least, the cocoon stage of it. This seems to be my final chapter before my book is released before I *finally* go public about my connection with the Pleiadians. Barbara Marciniak in one of her books said "who on earth in their right mind is going to believe me", it is **exactly** how I felt, word for word, and it has taken me a very long process indeed of personal acceptance and I am now ready to go public with my truth. As The Pleiadians told me when I was twelve that I would write a book one day and they encouraged me to start then and there. I had no idea. I had no idea, of what it would mean, of what it would bring to me and others, of the journey it would take me on. But, finally, after a very long process, I'm ready, I'm ready to take my next step, finally.

Chapter 10

Age Sixteen

Freedom at Sixteen

So the day of my sixteenth birthday arrived, so
long overdue. I was finally free, free to leave,
free to escape all the abuse. I did so on my
sixteenth birthday. I had waited so many years,
too many. There were times when the only
things that got me through were Jesus, The
Pleiadians, meditation and my spiritual books,
that contained within them much knowledge and
wisdom, the kind of education that I hungered for.
But it wasn't even just education, they had
become more of a survival crutch for me, as they
kept me safe in the understanding that the
esoteric, spiritual worlds are fact and not fiction or
childhood imagination and it hadn't been
imagination that had saved my life at the age of
twelve. My own guides and helpers and
especially The Pleiadians were educating me
directly, speaking to me directly and relaying all
the information and education that I would ever
need. But, still, I enjoyed the books and found
comfort in them knowing that I wasn't alone and
the only one having these kinds of experiences,
which helped me very much, as I was mostly told
not to speak about them to other people. I still do
enjoy my books, often finding some real
diamonds amongst them. They took me into a

world, where I wasn't the only one who had all this knowledge, though I hardly spoke of it at all much, except at those times when I felt compelled, times when I had been shown in order to help and make a difference; like the dream of my mum being attacked. So it was with much eagerness, anticipation and hunger, quite literally, that I waited and waited to leave. For me, it seemed like an eternity.

Finally, the day had dawned for me to just be myself, without pain being inflicted by others, often my own family. I walked out early in the morning ready to greet my new dawn, eagerly, with much anticipation. I took a small bag with me with only my most treasured possessions, which hadn't amounted to much at all. This was only the beginning of a new dawn, both internally and externally. In my mind's eye, I waved goodbye, silently I said goodbye to my family and left but it felt more like escaping and freedom. Freedom.

Sometime between the age of twelve and sixteen (probably when my stepdad started to lock me in my bedroom), I had begun to feel like a prisoner in my own home. I had a good 4 years of that feeling, so when my sixteenth birthday came, it really did feel like I was escaping from some sort of prison that had been made for me.

Chapter 11

The Pleiadian Memories

Something Happened

Something happened to me when I first sat down with my laptop to write about my many psychic experiences as a child. I started to channel information that did not come from my every day physical knowledge but which came from a higher place, from The Pleiadians, though I didn't realise it at the time. It was not my intention to channel information, I only intended and planned to write about my own psychic experiences as an Indigo child, as a child of abuse. Once I had started to channel information, I couldn't stop. This book is my own true experiences but it also has channelled information from a higher source, things of a spiritual nature etc., things I alone do not know. So it is a mixture of memories and channelled information from the Pleiadians. It may be my own higher self, spirit guides, angels, or some other higher knowledge or being but it was not from me, much to my own amazement. It was a wonderful experience and continues to be so, which fills me with a great feeling of internal peace, very similar to meditation. The information came so fast and thick I had trouble keeping up with the information, I was typing ten to the dozen on autopilot. I was making many spelling errors, I couldn't type quickly enough, as the information was coming so thick and fast I couldn't keep up, it was like taking a dictation (I have heard that said before by others who have also channelled information from a very high source indeed!)

I will continue to write for a mixture of reasons, partly to recreate that feeling of peace within myself, to share my experiences, to share my own knowledge, but more importantly to share the knowledge of channelled information from The Pleiadians, because it is very important to get that information out there into the wider public domain, I believe I'm channelling this information because the knowledge *needs* to be known. Many of us, in fact, all of us have gifts and abilities that lie dormant, undiscovered and unknown. Some of us find them, some of us don't, whether they are playing tennis or writing, whether they are spiritual or not.

The feeling, when I first started writing, was truly amazing and unique to me. I had not experienced anything like it before, during all my years of meditation and connecting with the spirit realms. It left me feeling on a high, full of energy on a much higher frequency or vibration than I had ever achieved before. It left me feeling full of energy, I felt amazing, alive, full of life, radiant, as if I had been zapped or plugged into a spiritual socket. During this time, I was also given information as to how to continue to keep the energy on an even keel and to keep my own energy vibrations pure, so that this state of energy could continue and grow on a stable level, rather than plummeting or skyrocketing. I was told to stop eating junk foods, I had to drink lots of water, and eat anything pure in nature, preferably organic as it is much purer, with lots of vegetables, in other words, a very wholesome pure diet. This was to help with the shift in myself that had occurred. All in all this, continued constantly for about two weeks until it felt like the elastic band snapped and I suddenly found myself operating at my normal lower level of energy, unfortunately for me.

I am still learning (as I write this) to control my own conditions in order to channel. By that, I mean I am learning to raise my own vibrations, without meditation in order to channel information, rather than something that just happens to me when I sit down to write. I have some control as to what happens (with regards to my opening and closing to channel) so that it is not just a sporadic thing that happens to me.

Having channelled information when I started to

write, I have since realised that, actually, I have been channelling information for myself for a very long time, since I was very young. Because I didn't have any official schooling, I had to get my answers elsewhere, which I did, but I had thought previously that the answers I received were coming from my own intuition. For example, if I needed to find out information (often quickly) I would ask my own intuition and get the answer in my own head. I have since realised that the information I had previously thought came from my own intuition is not that at all, but it's channelled from a higher place energy/frequency/vibration from some energy or being that has far greater knowledge than I have. It has since unfolded that this information has come from The Pleiadians and I am still remembering more and more all the time. I have channelled a lot of information and spent the last four years on and off doing so. The following pages are some of my memories as far as I have remembered but I do know there is a lot more to come for me and, as I do so, as I regain and remember more, I hope to share it with you.

2009

In 2009, I began channelling The Pleiadians though, at the time, I didn't realise it was them. Quite honestly, if I had known, I wouldn't have been ready for them and would have run a mile and a half away from myself and the true nature of who I am. The years in between then and now have been busy, to say the least, I don't know how I've managed to fit it all in. But spirit time is much quicker than our own. When I go into this state of consciousness, I can spend an hour there and come back and only have been gone five minutes human time, and gathered a whole pile or heap of information about us, about humanity, about the earth, about plants, about animals, *about energy*. It all really does seem to come down to being all about energy and how it works, as all, everything is really just energy, whatever it is, from a grain of sand to a planet, to us, it's all just energy, whatever form it takes. It starts with energy.

The years in between 2009 and now have led me on a journey of personal discovery, or rather a journey of remembering so much, memories that lay dormant within me, largely because of the abuse and long lost memories, that I honestly thought I would never get back again. However, my lost memories are not what I thought they would be. I began to remember the Pleiadians who they were, what they showed me during my childhood, how they kept me safe, how I first fully and consciously remembered leaving my body and reconnecting with them at the age of eight, I began to remember so much. I remember that they have always been with me. I remembered that they have been with me since my youngest days and *even* before that, I remember a *feeling* of having been with them in the past. This would have been in-between lives, much like heaven. I remember them telling me so much, about Egypt and people who seemed to surround me as a child, I remembered the Nazca lines that they showed me, about Atlantis, about the great fire at Alexandria, I remembered very much. But I also doubted myself hugely: *"who in their right mind was going to believe me anyway"* is something I would often ask myself. In 2012, I began a Shamanic course. It was a long process for me to accept the reality of what was happening to me. I simply didn't feel worthy enough. I needed something big within me to *shift*. The Shamanic course uncovered and unearthed a lot of information and things for me and within me. It has been a long process and still continues.

Slowly, the memories came together, unfolded, and continue to do so. With the help of my Shamanic teacher, I remembered my First Flight Out at the age of eight and reconnecting with them, as my physical body lay on the floor being abused. When I became aware that it was The Pleiadians that I was channelling. I purposefully stayed well away from reading any material about them, or channelled through them in particular, Barbara Marciniak and Barbara Hand Clow, as I didn't want it to influence my words at all. Up until very recently, I've managed to do so. I recently read Barbara Marciniak's work. Something that penetrated deep into the heart of me was saying something that read similar to "Many people will begin to remember The Pleiadians during childhood". This struck a big chord within me and I felt some kind of release. I do not believe that I am the only person remembering the Pleiadians, I'm quite sure others do too, yet there doesn't seem to be anyone writing about this. So, please, if you are reading this and you have also have had memories, write them up and let people know. Let us do what we came here for. Have courage and strength in your life purpose in our life purpose. In this time of the great shift.

There will come a time soon, in ten or twenty years from now, when a whole mass of people from all walks of life, all colours, creeds, and backgrounds will remember who they are and where they came from. They too will also remember connecting with the Pleiadians and other star nations, as children. The Pleiadian children, will remember themselves in all their truth and wake up. They will step up publicly and speak out. I simply am one of the first. There are many who will follow. It will not be an easy journey for them but it must be done. "Our light can no longer hide in the shadows, it must be brought forth so that we can fully regain our power".

Atlantis

There was a time long ago when illness and disease didn't exist on the scale that they do today when we knew how to treat our bodies intuitively, a time when we were much more advanced spiritually and lived with nature rather than against it. It was a time when we cherished our earth and used its natural resources without corruption or greed, a time when we lived in Harmony with Mother Nature and cared about ourselves, each other, our surroundings and the earth, a time without the use of chemicals when we didn't create diseases.

This place was called Atlantis, I know that it did exist, not because I read about it in some book and chose to believe it. I have been very lucky and been shown many wonderful things while on my spiritual journey, through meditations, dreams, visions, and premonitions.   This has been one of them. As sure as I know I breathe, I know, because I have seen it in a meditation, plants looked different then, they were much bigger, completely pure and therefore had a much more powerful effect on our bodies. Crystals were used to treat our bodies and for relaxation and general well being, to cleanse our systems. We lived much longer than we do today. We were completely at peace with one another. We would never dream of hurting one another because we knew we would only be hurting ourselves. In one Temple that I experienced in the centre of the hall, there was a huge crystal on a table. This was a large temple without a roof and open to the natural elements. The entrance was made of large columns (Roman Style) with steps leading down to the water. It was an amazing place that was built for healing aptly called "The Healing Temple". The air was so pure that, today, it would probably have an effect on us today, as we are so used to breathing polluted air, especially in the cities.

I have already written above how I had a meditation in which I was able to witness Atlantis. What I didn't say however is the following.

I know, as an Indigo Adult, that Atlantis did exist. For a moment, I'm going to stop there and go back to the very beginning, as I have come to experience and understand it. In the Beginning, we were beings of light, without the physical limitations of a human body. Many people call this the soul and they are right. We communicated telepathically and many of us still do, (He/She just knew what I was thinking, I could tell). Often at times without any intention or plan of doing so. These beings of light that are our ancient ancestors came from a different planet, not earth. Some beings were more evolved than others, much like today. We had families, much like today, that remained together.

These beings of light are what is called consciousness and are all linked together, much like a chain.

Today, we (many of us) call higher consciousness God and it is God but it is also part of us. We are not separate from it. God is within all of us. There is no separation. It is Man who first wrote about God being separate, in the Bible. "Imagine God is the Ocean, we are the Individual droplets of water". Going back to the beginning, when we first descended onto earth in human form with a physical body, we did so to learn, progress and experience new things, in a new form, our physical bodies. It seems we have lost our way. Corruption, greed, and power have a big part to play in losing our way.

Some beings remained behind and continued to develop, without a human form. Today we call them Angels. Atlantis is a place we created on earth, it is also the same dwelling place of Adam and Eve, known as "The Garden of Eden", the place of man and woman in human form. God did create us in his/her own form. We are part of God, not separate. These are both correct, God created us and we created ourselves, all at the same time. This is possible as God/Consciousness is part of us and not separate.

This was a magical place of beauty, love, spiritual wisdom, harmony and profound ancient knowledge, a divine place that was literally "Heaven on Earth". Temples were made from light and sound, much in the same way as we created ourselves from beings of light. Much was known about sound and vibrations, colour, crystals, healing, chakras, auras, and energies etc. Light and sound, when these become very dense and heavy, become solid in form.

In the beginning, the process of creating ourselves took a long time to happen. It didn't just occur over-night. We, slowly, probably over centuries, became denser and denser until we created our own bodies. Yes, God did create us in his/her image. But remember we are part of God. We are part of the whole, even to this very day, when we depart, pass over, die, this is where we return to!

This is what Jesus was talking about when he said there is no death, that he was the son of God and created in his image. People were able to see, as many of the mediums today, in the same way, see dead people, except they are not dead just in a different reality. Jesus was a highly evolved spiritual being. Everything that we created at that time in Atlantis was of a very pure nature/energy, ourselves the earth we lived on, the air, plants, trees, birds, everything was a much purer higher frequency/energy. The air was so pure, the flowers and plants much larger than today with much stronger and more powerful healing properties. The healing temples had no roofs, with enormous crystals placed inside at their centre. They were usually built near water.

What happened in Atlantis? What went wrong? Other beings came in from a Lower Realm and took our energy away. They corrupted us slowly, slowly and individually, secretly, but on a massive scale. They developed secret societies that some today call the 'illuminate'. This took hundreds of years, as we slowly became denser and denser and moving further away from our origins.

I want to recap on what went wrong in Atlantis bearing in mind that our bodies were not created or designed to age in the same way that they do today. We did live much longer then and it was a very slow process when these other lower beings came to Atlantis in the same way that we did. When they corrupted us, that is when we really started to age and die much younger. Before this, we were able and supposed to live for hundreds of years.

Now I spoke before of coming to earth from a spirit form without a human body. We didn't come from the earth, so we didn't surround the earth (at that time) as spirits or souls, beings of light. We came from a different place in the universe that operates at a much higher frequency. These opposite beings were operating at a much lower frequency than us. Many stories of the Devil and Demons originate from this time. Hence, God is a being of Light, love and pure energy of consciousness. We must wake up fully and realise who we are. We are not separate from God but are part of him/her, universal energy, the divine spark within is God consciousness energy. Other dimensions and realms do exist and many people, including Indigos, are able to experience these different realities, as I myself have.

New York

I have been shown during a dream a huge tidal
wave (as many other people have also) hitting
New York, killing hundreds if not thousands of
people. This seemed to happen very suddenly
and the people were unaware of the danger until
the last five minutes or so. I hope I am wrong.
Time after time, I had this dream/premonition,
continually right up until my late thirties.

Beneath The Sphinx

The TV was on and my mum was in the lounge. I
walked in and caught sight of the news about
Egypt. Instantly, I was in a trance altered state, I
no-longer heard what the news was saying. I
was being told and shown, (my mum completely
unaware of what was happening to me)
information about the Sphinx and laying beneath
the right paw (if you are standing in front of it,
head on) steps going down and a secret
chamber. The head of the Sphinx was different

and should have been a lion's head, as it was originally in the beginning. There is a very important link between the Sphinx and Leo the Lion constellation. There was an entrance between the paws. "It is much older". Secret chambers lie beneath the Sphinx beneath the right-hand paw, as you face it, head on and stairs going down. "The Sphinx was built on an older site".

The Great Fire

The following came to me in a "so-called dream" I had when I was about eleven years old, except it wasn't just a dream I was being shown something of huge importance, while in this "dream state". It felt very much as if I had lived and witnessed this fire, which is quite possible. It felt more like a long distant memory.

A vast mass of greatly valuable information about our true origins had been recorded, collected and gathered over many years since the beginning of time. Most, if not all, was destroyed deliberately in a great fire to keep us from knowing the truth about who we are and where we came from. This was intentionally done by a secret group of men to keep us from knowing our truth. Again many believe that they still exist today, known as the Illuminati.

More recently, I've been shown that originally there were thirteen signs. This information was lost, destroyed, changed, during the destruction caused by the Great Fire at the library in Alexandria.

Thirteen

The following information was lost, destroyed, changed, during the destruction of The Great Fire in Alexandria.

- 13 Astrology Signs
- 13 Ancient Tribes
- 13 Crystal Skulls
- 13 Sacred Sites

- 13 Sacred Geometrical Shapes
- 13 Basalt Moai on Easter Island
- 13 Chakras
- 13 Aura Levels
- 13 Earth Chakras

It is important to note that during this time we are going through a shift, a raise in consciousness and, as we do so, we are becoming more aware. Things are changing for us Spiritual and Physically! Our DNA is changing and has changed already. Our frequencies are changing, our bodies are changing, our minds are changing, we are becoming more spiritual. We are waking up spiritually, and this is having an effect on us, on our bodies, and our minds. The chakras within our bodies have changed, our dormant chakras are now active. Our Aura is more active and stronger and has an extra layer that was dormant and has now become active. The sky is not the limit. We are not alone in the universe. This is happening to us now and has been prophesied. The time is now. Are you ready? We are waking up. All of the changes taking place within us are a build up, a prelude to what's to come. We are living in a multidimensional universe, we are not alone. There is much life in the universe and other planets. Only a poor man would think himself alone, but in truth, we are never alone. Our cosmic brothers and sisters are waiting and watching, waiting for us to wake up!

Dinosaurs

I once had a vision or two of Dinosaurs walking with Man, living and co-existing at the very same time. It is taught in our schools that this didn't happen, that we came much later on. It isn't true, we did walk with the dinosaurs. It is one of the visions that I have up, until recently largely kept to myself. I would have been called a nut at the very least had I disclosed it. Things have changed and science has come a long way. I have quite by chance, apparently, found that there is now much proof and evidence to support my early vision, of our living at the same time as the dinosaurs. So I stand firm in writing this, though I can fully accept it may be hard to grasp. The earth was once believed to be flat. That was the science of the day and, at the time, the accepted truth. You don't have to believe me, research it for yourself, there is so much evidence. Conditioning is a large part of our society, created to stop us thinking for ourselves and getting to the truth of things.

The Pleiadians have since shown me that what they showed me as a child, is correct. I asked them to validate it for me, given its nature.

"Dinosaurs were created by us as we could see man's future. They were created partly to help man's survival during the Ice Age. Man walked with the dinosaurs. During the time of Atlantis, lower energies came in from outside of earth's atmosphere, a different race of ETs came to claim earth's territory as their own. We knew this, we saw it coming. Earth was knocked off course and the poles shifted, creating an Ice Age. The catalystic event created darkness for some time. The earth had been shaken, quickly, suddenly and violently. In order for man to survive, they would need a strong diet, rich in nutrients. So we created the dinosaurs to sustain them. Man hunted and killed the dinosaurs *during* the Ice Age to survive. To sum it up, we created the dinosaurs, we knew that a lot of good nutrient rich food would be needed in large quantities by man, so we created the dinosaurs."

Footprints of dinosaurs and humans have been found, which were made at the same time. There is much evidence and proof of this. It is not shared with the masses, you have to look a little bit deeper to find it.

The Nazca Lines

Sometime in my early Twenties, I began attending spiritualist churches to develop my own mediumship and I continued within these groups/circles for a good ten years. Where ever I lived, (within the UK) I would go on a weekly basis; my dedication and commitment were strong and is stronger now than ever, to spirit and the spiritual/esoteric knowledge. Whilst living in Edinburgh, during a meditation, I was taken very deeply into a meditation state and shown the Nazca Lines. I was taken about one hundred or two hundred feet above the earth and was looking down upon them. I was being shown that they (The Nazca Lines) had been made by extraterrestrials, (Star nations). They had not been made by human hands. They had been made somehow from high above the ground and had a feeling that their machines or craft had helped to do this in some way from above the earth. As with so many of my spiritual experiences, I questioned everything and this was no exception. I had a subtle feeling/sense of a guide or spirit being with me and showing me the Nazca Lines, someone in the spiritual dimensions wanted to show me, let me experience this and the information shared. I'm still not sure who it was though, but am thankful that they did come forward and show me. I was stunned by this and, when I came out of the experience, I sat very quietly, hardly making a sound, observing, waiting, questioning, silent and still. Although I was questioning, this experience brought a deeper stillness and peace within me. When it came for my turn to speak about my meditation, I spoke very little about it, giving only the very basic information. Verbally, I was stomped on by one of the church members. She had no interest in or belief in listening to me. I felt totally dismissed and cut off by her. She had mocked me and my experience, so I kept silent. I began to question her and the "spiritualist" churches and, shortly afterwards found Buddhism. I turned towards it, with arms wide open, I soaked up all of the teachings I could like a sponge. I ended up living on Holy Island in Scotland, in a wonderful state of freedom and bliss most of the time.

More recently, I have been shown more information about The Nazca Lines. A catalystic event burnt them well into the earth, fire/heat during an event of devastation. There was a sense of destruction, panic and a feeling of dread at the time. I'm not sure why it was done, purposefully though I'm sure. These lines were burnt deeply into the land through intense heat/fire, involving a craft. This way a cataclysmic event that was caused/created by technology, far more advanced than ours is even today. The Nazca lines remain today only because of this event, burnt well into the land. My feeling is that they remain as some kind of map and warning of the past and what happened. I cannot say with certainty that these beings were benevolent or not. At an important time in Earth's history, this event happened, or they (the Nazca Lines) were created at this time but both are equally important events to our true history and the real history of the earth and our past.

Consciousness

"I am Infinite Consciousness. We are all Infinite Consciousness. The only difference is that I have realised it and you haven't".

This is a quote that I channelled in relation to the

following:

Look around you at today's world. What do you
see? Do you see love, peace, harmony, mothers
loving their children, a world in which we care
about each other, a world in which there is no war
because people are misguided into thinking that
the land belongs to them?   It doesn't belong to
them and it never has. You take a good look
around you, we live in a crazy world that is full of
corruption, greed, and poverty, a world full of Hell
and hellish things. On the flip side, we also live in
a world that is full of love and blessings, spiritual
people and places, It all depends on where we
are spiritually in our own growth. The internal
world represents and mirrors the external world.
Only three percent of our entire population is
spiritual but this is growing and expanding, as our
consciousness is growing and expanding, hence
our thoughts and feelings are changing our world.
As we change our own internal world, we change
the outer world. Nothing is more important than
first changing our own outlook, thoughts, and
feelings. A famous piece of music states "If you
want to make that change, start with the man in
the mirror". This piece of music that was sung by
Michael Jackson was indeed channelled
(probably unknowingly) from a source higher than
the person who wrote it.

Michael Jackson was a very spiritual person and very 'in tune'. Music has a very spiritual aspect and can reach out to people far and wide. His life was predestined (I believe) so that he could reach people on a spiritual level and open their eyes and he did this through his music. I truly believe the vast majority of his music was channelled. Whether he wrote it or not, it ended up in his lap and was able to reach people in that way. I myself have suffered much abuse of all kinds including sexual. Yet, not for one minute, do I believe at all that he was a child abuser, ever. I do, however, believe that a part of his downfall was the Media, who intentionally set out to topple him, as they have done many times with others. I also believe there are some people that the media, no matter how hard they try, cannot topple. A mass of people do not buy into this, and his fans have shown this. He was a very spiritual person, almost magically and had a deep understanding of spiritual laws.

I have experienced God and infinite consciousness because I'm part of him/her, The Universal Energy, Divine Light, Buddha, Krishna, Mother Mary, Jesus, Mohammed, Archangel Michael. It is all part of the same thing, energy, divine pure conscious energy and we all are a part of it, all of us. There is no one with a human body who is not. Okay, let me explain it another way in very simple terms God (or whatever you choose to call it) is the Ocean, we are the single droplets of the Ocean. We are not separate from it but part of it.

Whether you like it or not, this is how it is and science is now proving it. Just take a moment to think about that. You are part of God, you are not separate. So you say you love God, then you need to start loving yourself. When you love yourself, then you will really love God because you are of the same energy, consciousness. You are infinite consciousness and so is God. When we realise that we are all connected, we are the same energy that has been divided into individual separate parts. We are the same, you and I. When people realise this, that is the time when we will have peace and wars will stop. They will and we can guarantee this will happen.

Some years ago, I was doing a course where I met a woman who was on the same level of frequency as me, someone who I connected well with. We were doing the course (I am still friends with her today). Well, during the events of the day, I looked into her eyes and I saw myself. Now that was very profound for me and you may not understand this at first. The reason I saw myself in her eyes is very simple. She is part of me and I of her. We are droplets of the same ocean. There is no place where you begin and I end, we are all connected, we are all of the same stuff, we are all from the same ocean of consciousness.

I was not conditioned the same way as other children are today and they are conditioned to follow the herd. I have chosen not to do that. I have chosen my own path. When you choose your own path, that is when you are truly free.

Right now, we want to talk about being conditioned in today's society especially about children. Especially, if they are gifted and if you are a gifted child in today's world, God bless you. We must talk about taking your children out of school if you love them, not because you want them to be uneducated but because you want them to be educated and spiritual leaders. You will have to trust that there are other schools available like the Steiner schools and others. You can also educate them at home, get home tuition but if you continue to send them to school, you are not helping them. You are teaching them to be conditioned as you were as your parents were as their parents were. If you want to do something to break the cycle that has been created for us our in heavily conditioned and controlled world. If you love your children and want them to be educated about the world and you believe the teachings of, say for example Gregg Braden, David Icke, Doreen Virtue etc.

I once knew a woman who claimed to have a love for birds. Yet, she chose to keep them in her home in tiny little cages. That's not loving, that's ownership. We don't own anything, not our children and not mother earth, nor do we have control over mother nature, not in the way the mainstream thinks we do.

The Greys

I had recently moved to Galway; and had been here a few months in 2009, when I had a "dream", one of my real dreams as I call them. They are real and take place on the astral plane or higher dimension where our spirit exists with or without our bodies. I was up above the earth in a circular ship, lying on a table that was at my waist height. My feet and hands were in some kind of cuffs or restriction, tied to the table. I felt much fear and panic, as I couldn't move. There were other people in the room in the same position as I was and they seemed to be spaced out about ten feet apart from each other. I wasn't able to lift my head up and have a good look around but I'm not sure if my head had been tied, restricted down as well. I could hear their cries of pain. I thought I was in danger, as the other people most definitely were. Three beings appeared around me, two on my right and one on my left, short in height and naked with large almond-shaped eyes. They didn't seem to be threatening *to me*. They were doing some kind of test on me and the others. I heard one of them speak, yet no sound came from their mouths but still, it spoke, so I can only gather that it must have been telepathically. I heard one of them say that "this one's different", meaning me. I was pleading with them to let me go, without any kind of experiment being done on me, as they were doing to the other people in the room. There was a strong sense of panic and an eerie feel, a sense of pain seemed to be lingering in the air, of what was to come. I could not seem to wake up and get back into my body. I could not bring back my conscious awareness back *into* my body, which I had learned to do over the years, given all the astral plane experiences I've had, I'd learned to do this, but in this situation, I couldn't. I wasn't in control. It wasn't until recently I realised what this meant. It meant that those beings had control over my consciousness and I didn't. They were not deliberately trying to hurt any of us, I felt, or cause us any harm or pain, not intentionally. Their main aim and focus was to learn about us and gain valuable information about us, our bodies and our DNA. I felt that their sole purpose and aim was to carry out experiments on us, or rather the other people in the room. My attention was brought back to the being speaking that "I was different" from the others. I felt my panic diminish and knew I would be safe and free from harm or any type of experiment.

I awoke in the early hours of the morning. It took me up now (June 2013) to realise the full implications of this event and I've never spoken of it to anyone, before writing this. These beings, I believe, are extraterrestrials. They were small, short, naked with large almond shaped eyes and protruding round little tummies. The importance of this meeting with them must have had some connection with the Pleiadians surely?

Since then it has come to my attention that these beings are known as the Greys. They were not cruel beings, intent on causing pain. Their only aim, focus, and mission was to conduct experiments for gathering information, much like science. They had a real feel for science and discovery going on for them and they were very interested in us and seemed oblivious to the pain or cries that people gave out. It was more from a scientific point of view that they seemed to be interested in us. It felt more like they had a job, a mission to do regardless of how we felt or any pain inflicted on us. Had I not been different (And I still don't know how I was different) and recognised as such and just within the nick of time, I know that I too would have ended up being just another experiment for them or of theirs. I don't know what happened to the others in the room, for when I heard the words "this one's different". I was allowed to go back into my body. And that scares me, the knowledge that some other being had control over my consciousness. I had never known that before, not in the way I was experiencing it. It is the only astral plane experience I've ever had, where I was not able to re-enter my physical body, which means they had control over my consciousness and where it went and I had never experienced that before. I hadn't known it was possible until then. And I believe that needs further investigation of some kind. When I say investigation, I mean finding answers, without causing pain, of any kind, to anything or being. It is also a question that I will myself be asking the Pleiadians.

The Human Heart

The human heart is not designed to be caged and love only one person. It is meant to soar, reach out and fly and love many people, in truth and purity, on all levels, in different ways. The way you love your father is different to the way you love your mother, yet both are your parents, both have equality and equal standing in your heart. The same is true of sexual relationships. You were not designed to be contained by the heart to love only one person in your entire lives. You were meant to share, reach out, fly, soar and love many people equally in different ways. I'm not speaking of lust, I'm speaking of love, pure love from the heart. Desire and lust are something completely different, that is not love at all. It is sexual desire, not love as I mean it, in its purest form, marriage and the way its been made by religion is not the way it is meant to be, that is why so many get divorced today. They know it's no longer right for them, so they move on and eventually meet another life partner.

The human heart was designed to be as free as the human mind, only it has been taught by society and its structures not to be free, to be contained, to follow its rules, to love only one for life. It has been taught to follow its rules that are the very opposite of the truth of God. I did not create you for that, that is non-sense. I created you for you to love, have joy, experience, share, love with all of your heart, love in all different ways. Marriage was born from religion, it was not my plan, it was made a rule of religion and man, it is not my rule, it is the very opposite is my plan.

Why do relationships hurt so much when they end? Why has my heart and soul felt like it has been ripped apart? It is caused by the fear of letting go and letting be, in other words, attachment. It is impossible for the *normal* person to love a partner without attachment because your society dictates this, it even commands it. When spiritually aware people love, they have no attachment or a greatly reduced attachment. They understand attachment for what it is, a false thing. Spiritually aware people let things, events, come and go, let it be, be in the now, as much as possible for them the spiritual people. So they have a much easier time, with less pain and the heart*ache* of letting go, letting be. They do not cling or fight or try to stop things. They don't try and control things, events, relationships. Your preachers are not men of God. They are men of illusions and some of them are deceptive but most of them have come under the spell of illusion themselves, as they were taught, as their sons were taught and so on.

The spiritual man does not follow a religion, he follows God. The two are often opposite extremes, you only need to look at what religion has done to man, in the name of God to understand this. God would never hurt man, for he is Man, some men understand this but they are not religious, they are the spiritual man, they are the truth, the way, but you must not follow them either, not completely, not without question. Indeed do not follow *anything* without question, for without questioning everything, you cannot learn or understand anything. You must follow your own path.

What should I call this book? "Fear of God."

There was a time when religion put the "fear of God" into Man, in my name. That is not my name. They rose up to control man in the fear of God but it was an illusion for their own gain, greed, power and they called it religion and so was born "the wrath of God" but it goes against me. It goes against God and all that "I am". It is not the truth, it goes against me and all that I am.

It was an army of people putting the fear into man "fear God" or else he (God) will strike you down. God does not create fear, man creates fear in God's name. "Thy will be done" but it is not in my name, it is from his own fear, illusion and the conditioned self, conditioned by the very society that created the illusions of who I really am, much like a smoke screen.

Why me for writing these words?

If not you then who? You are pure of heart and you know it, you have been called that by your own guides for a long time now. And yet still you doubt. I am God and I am here. I am all around, inside and outside you. I am God, I am Man, I am all energy that exists on earth and around it, I am pure conscious thought. I am the divine spirit of all living things. No 'thing' exists outside of me, even the dark. I am the opposite of myself, that which you call evil so that I can experience myself in all my entirety of who I really am. In order for me to understand that which I am, I need to experience that which I am not, and so the pendulum swings back and forth in the wind.

I recently heard "God is in the garden"

Where else would I be?

I am all that is, I am everywhere inside and out, you may even find me in a church.

That's funny!

I even enjoy laughter and have a sense of humour.

There are many different peoples in the world, many different cultures, races, nations, colours and creeds, nationalities. As many as there are of those, the same for spiritual awareness and consciousness can be said. Spiritual people, awareness, and consciousness have many different levels/layers and groups, soul groups that connect. Any group of people "that connect" do so on a higher level, on a spiritual level, they can "feel it". They feel connected to each other, hence "soul mate" and soul groups. Spiritual people connect from a heart level of feeling. That which you are, you attract, like attracts like. The universe is a mirror. This is why "normal" people don't get you because they are operating on a different level of consciousness, their own level. They have not yet raised their own level of awareness to reach mine, as you have and many spiritually aware or consciously aware people like you are, and many others before you, and many others still to come in future time as man understands time.

Your level of awareness is greater than that of most people in "normal" ordinary society who fill their days with nonsense. They are not concerned with the spiritual, as you are first and foremost, they are concerned only with material gain. That will not always be the way, it will soon change and change it will. The whole of humanity is changing, can you not see it? Can you not feel it?

I feel it and I have a sense that it's changing and something is shifting, on an energetic level.

Let me put it into words you will understand. For a long time, my pendulum has been swinging back and forth. It is coming soon to a time when it will be in balance, it will be at the centre, at the heart, in harmony with all of creation, all that I have created. All of humanity will be in harmony with all of humanity and all that is, all that I am. Not one thing will exist on earth that is not in harmony with all that is. A time of great love is coming, love of all, for all, from all, no negative emotion will be felt. It is coming. It is changing. Can you not feel it?

It is the end of a cycle and the beginning of a new one. It is indeed A New Dawn, a new age The Age of Aquarius. Can you not feel it?

I do, I do feel it but I also feel a lot of fear from people/media about the coming changes. People are scared.

Fear of the unknown has always existed. Man does not know God, so he fears him. Spiritual people do not fear the changes coming to earth, they know and have known God. Normal people, as you put it, need to follow the spiritual people/teachers and that will lessen their own fear.

But you said, "Don't follow any teachers?"

Don't follow blindly and always question everything. But all people on earth can feel, sense that something is coming, something is changing and shifting. Normal people need to embrace and surround themselves with the spiritual ones, the enlightened beings and this will help to raise their own awareness/vibration and lift away from their own fear. This, in turn, will speed things up, help things along as you understand it. It is like a domino effect. Indeed, I created the domino effect in all its simplest terms, for you all, to understand spiritual laws simply.

I still doubt.

It will not always be so. All of you are changing, you have raised your consciousness and awareness. All of humanity can feel this. All of humanity is raising its awareness. A huge shift is coming and doubt will cease. Have you not heard it said, "That a butterfly on one side of the earth can be felt on the other?"

Yes, I have.

All energy is connected, like a spider's web. When one shifts you all shift. I am the voice you heard before in your room, do you remember?

How could I ever forget?

Some people forget they forget who they really are.

I am God, the same voice you heard before. I will come again and lift the veil.

Can I see you, God?

You will never see God, that which I am for I don't have one face. I am all energy in its highest form, its truest form. I am faceless. But you can hear me and will continue to do so. You can feel me, can you not?

I can.

And you know that I am with you in all ways, you can feel it.

I can.

So know that I am with you, inside and outside, in all ways, I am energy, I am God the divine source.

Many people, before you and long after you, will show me to others in different ways, through writing, through songs, music and many more ways. But you will never ever see me, for I am faceless but I work through many people and have done so, even those who still doubt their own divinity and God-like oneness. They doubt their own minds you still do, although that feeling is becoming less and less with you, as it is all the same for the whole of humanity. A great shift is coming, a great dawn, a new dawn, a new age. Who do you think coined that term "a new age". Yet again, man has come up with negative connotations for this term. It is not new, it is as old as I am, the dawn of time.

Religion has a lot to answer for, as does society and humanity but that is changing. It will change, it will come to pass. Many people have preached my teachings before, Buddha, Jesus, Moses, Levi, Sufi, Morpheus.

The great teachers that speak my name, of me, will never cease, they will only ever increase and increase and increase until the people will hear the word of God and not the word of man. They will not fear, they will not doubt and the way will be clear.

A new dawn is indeed coming. Do not fear it, my children, but rather embrace it, feel it and grab it with both hands wholeheartedly and allow it. It will raise your consciousness and that of all humanity. That which is being written by the great spiritual teachers today, about 2012 and changes is true. A new dawn is coming and so it is written.

Chapter 12

The Pleiadians Channelled

The Veil Begins To Lift

I was sent an unexpected email by a guy in America, asking me to work with him. Yet, he did not explain how I would be doing this and he gave me no clues. To be honest, I initially thought he was a bit of a nut job. I have since completely changed my mind. I re-read the email several times pondering over it carefully on the Friday when I had received it. On Saturday, I was on Facebook and we got chatting. I then started to channel a group of beings I had vaguely heard of before but knew about (or so I believed at the time) to my own amazement, bewilderment, and disbelief. However, as I had been open to channelling through writing before, I was open to receive. While I was doing so and in the moment, I did not question it, I was merely a channel for the information to come through. It was afterwards that the shock started to hit me. I had so much doubt, not about channelling because I knew that to be true, but rather I doubted very strongly that it was coming from the Pleiadians.

On the following Sunday, I was booked into a one day workshop which involved a Shamanic

Journey. It was during this first Shamanic journey that I had an incredible experience and my memories of The Pleiadians being with me as a child began to emerge and continue to do so.

A New Dawn

PS refers to the Pleiadians and CN refers to Carol Noonan.

PS

"A New Dawn means A New Dawn for Humanity, spiritually. We told you before (Carol) that we would explain to you the full meaning behind that phrase. It has great meaning and it means that spiritually, man is now evolving, consciously. It is all about spiritual growth, that is why so many humans are channelling us, (you ask and we answer) because man is progressing spiritually and becoming *more* aware, therefore more open to us, and all Star Nations. We are the bringers of the dawn. We are here to help you, to assist you, during this great time on earth, in earthly man's evolution, (that is an answer for JS and KH). Man is shifting consciously, progressing spiritually and that is why we are here, to help you on this great journey. It is part of a great contract, of our contract that we made together, at the time of Atlantis. We made a bond, a pact. We bring forth ourselves to help you, to assist you in your spiritual development.

We have been waiting a long time. We bring forth great joy and we rejoice. The heavens opened up and rejoiced. This has two meanings and again we will explain the greater meaning of that to you (Carol) in the future, as we continue to build our relationship. You have been on a journey of personal growth, so we stepped back from you, Carol. It is now time to step forward again and again and again and again but Carol, we will do this slowly, your energy, your physical body needs time to adjust to all the physical "stuff" and changes that you have been through over the last few months, you need time Carol. We will come again to you and we will rejoice but for now, we must go. And, yes, you Carol will board our craft in love and safety for we know how very important this is for you. We will show you all and teach you about how our crafts/ships work, the technology we have. This we promise, in the love, light, and safeness, that you need Carol.

Before we told you about the scholars and such people, that you would be well known throughout the world, sought out, and asked many, many questions. Some of this is about our craft but, mostly about our technology. Only, when Man is ready and developed enough spiritually, will we give it. Otherwise, man would abuse our technology, as indeed he has done in the past. He has greatly abused it for evil purposes. We go now. Rest in peace and love. We love you. Before we go "Yes" we have been with you since you were a child, helping you to build your energy, to stay conscious. That is one of the reasons why your spiritual experiences have been so thick and fast like boom, boom, boom, one, two, three. We love you and we go, back to the heavens from whence we came."

The Pleiadians Channelled

"The word "God" in the Bible should be replaced with the word "Gods" and then things would make much more sense to you. And the Gods created us in their own image."

The Channel Opens and the Questions Begin

PS

The word God in the Bible should be replaced with the word Gods. That was the way, that was the truth and The Gods came down from the heavens and the sky opened up. And The Gods said 'let there be Light' and there was light. And the Gods created us in their own image and man was born. As we said before and we say it again, over and over to many. Some continue to ignore us because of fear, as you have, but that is changing. Ask and you shall receive.

CN

I am ready and I have many questions for you.

PS

So let us begin our journey together for we have been waiting for you a long time. We have come to you before and this you remember. You have seen glimpses of us throughout your entire life and sometimes you have forgotten these events, like a long distant memory. But you are ready now.

CN

Yes, I am ready

PS

So let us begin, please.

CN

But please wait.

PS

Why?

CN

Well, I have much fear.

PS

Fear is an illusion.

And so let us begin our journey together. Let us blend our energies more and more.

CN

I am ready now to begin, my Gods.

PS

Do not hold back (through fear) what you shall receive or it will be lost, and important things/knowledge will be lost as it was before in the Bible and other books and music. Enjoy this journey.

CN

My first question is who are you, really? I had so much doubt, but I have so much less now though I can also feel it lingers in the background of my conscious mind. I do feel it will all change and the heavens shall open up and you will pour your streams of light, awareness and conscious thought from yourself into me. I shall be held in a stream of light while you do this?

PS

Yes, that is the way it will be. These streams of light, as you call them, are real and have existed for aeons of time. They have been seen by many and photographed. They are one way of how we connect with you

Who are we? We are The Pleiadians and our sister/brother planet Sirius also wants to blend with you very much and you can feel them hovering in the background somewhere just behind us. In your mind's eye with your third eye, you can even see us.

CN

Yes, I can.

PS

Then, let us blend now fully.

In the beginning, we came from our planet and we created Man in our image and likeness. As we saw ourselves. We walked with the apes and communicated with them, we created them. Then we created Man in our own image, we are the Gods, we are the illumed ones, we are the ones you have been waiting for. *You* are the ones you have been waiting for. We have been waiting for you. And you have been waiting for us. We are here to blend, we are here to help you remember who you are, you are Gods among men and we walk among you and the Gods came down from the heavens and Man was born in our image. We say this again and again to many in many ways and yet many still ignore us. We love you so much and have so much to share. So much knowledge has been lost, hidden, destroyed, forgotten. Fear, doubt, illusion have risen and controlled by those, less wise shall we say. Corruption, greed, fear, doubt, illusion, have controlled man for long enough now, enough, enough already. Your world is changing. The shift is coming and it is happening now. It is no illusion, it is happening, can you not feel it, can you not see it all around you? And so can others, humanity, as you know, is changing and we are helping you and all humans and humanity to shift, shift up a gear or two or three or four. Your consciousness is rising and so is all of humanity. Let go of fear and doubt and, as you do this, you will let go of fear, doubt, and illusion and you, too, will become illumed and enlightened. These two words are directly intertwined and have much the same meaning.

CN

Wait, please slow down. You are downloading information to me so fast, I get it and I trust it (well kind of) but what you have just shown me will take pages and pages, perhaps even a whole book.

PS

Yes, we know. Take your time and keep asking the same questions, if you need to. That is okay with us. At least, you are listening to us now and writing it down and remembering who you are. So don't worry about asking the same questions again and again. It is okay with us. We are very happy, pleased and even delighted that you are doing so. Now that you are aware of us, we are not going anywhere and will continue to work with you. Do not worry that we will disappear from you again, that will not happen. We will be with you always. You can call on us, whenever you want or need. Now that we have/are building up our relationship we will never leave you ever and when you pass over to the world of spirit, we will be waiting for you then.

CN

You will be meeting me when I die? I have been working as a medium for some years now, so I understand the death process, how our loved ones pass over into the spirit world. But you will be waiting for me also?

PS

Yes, we are your parents we love you. There is no difference. In fact, we are closer to you than your own parents, who are much further from you than even you realise. You have been working in the spirit realms more of your life than you have not, you are closer to us than your own parents, who do not love you in the same way as we do, unconditionally.

CN

Are you talking about me as an individual or as humanity?

PS

No, just you. You might as well have been raised as an only child, as an orphan. Tell us where were your parents? You know your childhood situation and you don't have to share it yet if you don't want to. The time will come for you to also publish that book when you are ready. And so, yes, we will be waiting for you as any loving parent would. We know you don't doubt that.

CN

I have so many questions for you, probably hundreds, I don't know where to start?

PS

Let us start with the streams of light we were explaining just now. The streams of light are very real and have been photographed, videoed and seen by many, many people for aeons of time. They are more than just streams of light, as a normal person would see them through the naked eye. They are one way we have of connecting with you, but not the only way. We have been doing this for aeons of time since we first came to the planet that you call earth, but we will talk about that later. So let us continue with the stream of light for now. Contained within that light is our calling telepathically to you humans. It is a signal to say are you coming? It contains a wealth of information from us to you, such as are you coming? are you ready? We are here, it is to let you know that we are simply waiting until you are ready. Know that that time is now. The Mayans speak of it as other great ancient peoples do, a beam of light.

CN

Okay, so it is one way you have of communicating with us?

PS

Yes, but it is not the only way. We have many ways. Do you want to hear them?

CN

Oh, yes. Of course, I do...I see that you have a sense of humour...I also "see" that you radiate even more light and a feeling of love when you are most happy.

PS

We do indeed. It is our source of being, the same as yours. Only yours is in the heart and spiritual soul. You humans radiate out just as we do, only you do it in a different way. You use a different method/system to ours. We do not have bodies as such, loosely speaking.

CN

But I can "see" you with my third eye and have a sense/feeling that you have a body. If you don't, then what am I seeing?

PS

Our essence that radiates out from within us...we just have a different system. Let us explain more, so you will understand. We are light beings without a body. When humans die, they become light beings also without a human body, so that only the soul/spirit exists. You have known that since a child. Well, we never had a body in the first place. When you mediums see spirit, you see a "body" and get their essence/soul and you see them as they were on the earth...well, that is the same with us...we "See" our individual essence of who we are with a body, but we are without bodies. You simply see our soul/spirit. In the beginning, you didn't have a body the spirit came first. You know that we have told you before.

CN

Yes, I remember. How could I ever forget, except when I have?

PS

Good, we see that you have a sense of humour and that is good for building the relationship between us. We are so pleased you are finally listening. It took a long time and difficult journey, did it not? We feel your pain of the past and are most sorry, but you do know that it brought you here today, in all its entirety. Don't you?

CN

Yes, I do, I wouldn't change it, even if I could. It was the way it was meant to be. It was the way I designed it.

PS

Yes, we are aware that you now work with the power of thought and its creative force, whatever you want to call it, the law of attraction. Thoughts are creative, creating your own reality etc. etc.

CN

I have so many questions for you. The information you are giving me is coming so quickly I cannot possibly keep up at that speed. It will all take at least a book or several...

PS

Ask the questions that others (within society) would ask. And we will answer.

CN

Should we fear you? There is much fear of extraterrestrials in the world, fear of the unknown, fear that you will somehow hurt us and do experiments on us? That you would capture us, take us off somewhere and harm us?

Sunday 21st August 2011

PS

Let us draw closer and we will blend our energies again...open your heart, expand your consciousness...you know how to do this you have been doing it since you were a young child...others have seen that you are different and many have even been afraid of you and feared you and we know how that feels. So do not worry. We are with you guiding you along. We shall remain with you forever and we will be there when you depart from the physical body. We will be waiting with loving arms to welcome you into our world completely and that is where you shall stay for as long as you want.

CN

What about my question about fear?

PS

Why would you fear your parents? Okay, well you understand that your parents are an exception. Generally speaking, people don't fear their parents. We are your parents and we love you. It breaks our hearts when we try and connect yet fear stops you. We love you and

would never hurt you. We will go into this more.
We want to move on and talk about other things
for now. But we promise to answer all your
questions. Only you cannot receive all of the
information from us in one go. It would be too
much, too overwhelming for you to receive it all
together. You understand this, don't you? You
are aware that it would be too overwhelming for
your system to take it would cause you to
overload and dismantle.

CN

Yes, I am aware of that. Thank you for putting
me first before the information, I know how
important it is to get it out there, people need to
know, need to know many things, that you are
loving beings of light and you would never harm
us.

PS

Okay, so let us go back to what we have shared
with you, in-between the times when you were
channelling us, but not writing it down. You still
remember, don't you?

CN

I do, yes, most of it. Please explain to me again,

fully, so that it will be well readable for others. And share what I was shown during my Shamanic Journey on that Sunday when I was left with no doubt.

PS

Okay, let us begin.

CN

It has taken only seconds for you to show me information that will take many days to write. I cannot possibly keep up with you.

PS

Take your time. It's okay. You have the rest of your life to do so.

Yes, God does exist. He exists in the way you understand him. But others do not. You understand him to be like the ocean and the individual droplets of water, to be each individual human among you. And that is correct in your understanding, God is you, you are God, God is within you, not outside you he is all the energy that is. He can be found in all energy and matter. There is nothing that exists outside God, not even us, not even us. Though we are from a different planet we are all made up of the same energy.

Let us explain so that you will understand. God is the ocean and the individual droplets of water are individual humans. It will not take much imagination for you to know, to understand. There are several oceans on your planet, that is how you can understand how we are also part of God and you, we are all the same energy you, I and God, just operating at different frequencies. Energy is not confined to the earth, it is a cosmic energy. It is a cosmic life force that connects us, even us, who are from different planets even different galaxies. The God energy is not separate from cosmic energy. It is from the same source.

CN

Wow, Oh My God, that is amazing. I'm stunned, stunned into silence.

PS

Yes, that is right, my dear one, my pure of heart, your guides have called you that for a long time now. God, as you call it/him/her, was created before the big bang. God "was" the big bang, which was an energy force, a force of energy that came to know itself and then exploded or imploded onto/into itself. And hence energy was born. It was a great time, a time of the beginning when matter was created from energy. But the energy existed *before* the big bang. It came to know itself as an energy force and then exploded/imploded and matter was born.

CN

So God existed before the big bang?

PS

Yes, that is correct. Energy existed before the big bang but it evolved and formed matter. It formed the universe's galaxies and planets. It created everything that exists, *everything*, every single living thing, all energy comes from God, even those, that cannot be seen with the human eye.

The energy that you call God became aware of itself…

CN

Okay, I get it, but what about before, before the big bang and even before that time, when energy became aware of itself, what about that time?

PS

It is ongoing, exploding and imploding constantly, only it takes millions of years to do so. The energy *is always* contracting and expanding and then exploding, imploding. *Always,* never ceasing. It is an endless cycle of life, death, and birth, the same as for humans and reincarnation, the same for cosmic energy, planets and galaxies, stars and light systems. It is a continual system, never ending, only going through different stages, contracting expanding forever, on and on it goes. It will never end. And, what's more, before the big bang, there were planets and galaxies and stars and many beings all over the place and light beings...

CN

Stop, hold on, please...so what your saying is...

PS

We are saying that everything that exists today in your galaxy, stars, planets, universes and light beings, have all existed before. Humans experience reincarnation, life, birth, death, and that is also true for the universes and galaxies, it is true *for all life*. God created everything, all matter and it is *all governed* by the same laws, the same natural laws. It has even existed several times before, as humans have, as above, so below. There is *so much* that your science does not understand. There is also *much* that is hidden from the masses. Science is way ahead, way ahead of what you believe it to be, or are being told (by a huge distance). Science knows a whole lot more than it is sharing today with the masses. The governments know that there is life on other planets, they know that "extraterrestrials" exist. They know this because we have shown them many times but they choose to keep it secret.

CN

Hold on, the governments know that extraterrestrials exist?

PS

Yes, of course, they do, it is *top secret* to them though. They are not willing to share their knowledge for fear of many uprisings around the globe. They have many "meetings" about this, many talks and discussions. Much research into science is much more evolved than you are told. It even has machines that can space travel, what you would call UFO's? Governments all over the world do not share what is really going on, they keep so much from you, largely for fear of a global uprising, except that has started to happen anyway, regardless. It is part of the raising of your human consciousness, but we will talk about that later.

We have been "visiting" you since the dawn of time. In fact, we are the Gods that created you in the first place. We came from the heavens and created you in our likeness.

CN

Woooow, there slow down....I am starting to understand this, but many will not. We people are taught that God created us in his likeness.

PS

No that is partly incorrect, yet it is true also, it is a complex subject. God created all of us, he created us and then we created you. We walked this planet you call earth long before human "evolution", which, in truth, as science has tried to explain it, is not correct at all. Forget science. It is always changing its mind and finding new discoveries, ideas and concepts all the time. When man's "science" understands the spiritual laws, then he should apply those laws to science and not the other way around, as he has been continually trying to do for decades. It is rather futile, like trying to fit a round peg into a square hole. It does not fit. Science has little understanding of the spiritual laws, but that also is untrue and incorrect. What you are told and taught by science is known to be incorrect, yet it is still being taught. The gap between the spiritual laws and science is much, much closer than you are being told. A huge amount of information is used kept from you. And, yes, the governments are very much aware of us. In fact, we have communicated with them more than once, they know we are real and exist. There is no doubt among them. But there is much fear and control of the masses going on. Fear, power, greed, and corruption, amongst other things, are rampant. Many experiments are held in secret.

Let us move on, for we do not wish to create fear either. We are simply here to guide you as a human race for we are your parents, your cosmic parents and we created you in the beginning.

We walked the earth at the time of your so-called "evolution". We came down from our planet and walked on planet earth, we took the hands of the monkeys and walked together speaking to them telepathically. We told them what we were doing, that we were going to create a new human race on earth, to prepare them.

CN

But, hold on, I was told before that we came from the spirit world and then came into being in our physical bodies to experience life on earth in the physical form. Is that wrong?

PS

No, it is correct. We merely assisted but it is a complex law. You can have more than one segment of an orange but it's still an orange.

CN

Hold on, I'm confused. Why should we need your help? Spirit is ever powerful, needs nothing, can go anywhere, and do anything, it does not need assistance.

PS

Do you think that the "spirit" you speak of was just aimlessly circling and hovering above and around the earth? No, it came from a different planet. It came from different planets, not only The Pleiadians but also from other planets in the universe. We were not the only ones. There was a great war going on at the time that we chose earth. It was called a "war of the worlds". Many planets were at war with each other. There was one planet, in particular, that had a much lower vibration/frequency what you would call "negative energy". They caused much trouble amongst many different "peoples" on neighbouring planets and eventually, they also came to earth. In fact, they came to earth at the time of Atlantis, and still walk among you. All you and your descendants come from the stars, you are extraterrestrials and you are stardust. We have tried and tried over the ages to try and draw close to you to help you remember who you are and where you really came from.

Let us go back to Atlantis.

Atlantis was a perfect place and then "negative energies" came in as you would call them. They had a different agenda, were corrupt, greedy and power hungry. The people in Atlantis at the time being so very pure in nature were not aware of what was happening or chose to ignore it. And before long Atlantis itself was full of deceit, corruption, greed and power hungry peoples. We do describe it as like an infection it spread across the land and people, like a disease. It caused disruption and fear and much unrest. That was part of the downfall of Atlantis. And to this day it is still happening to a lesser or greater degree at various times. None of your humans are actually from earth, they all came from different planets, in the beginning.

CN

But some people say that people lived in Egypt and that at that time we were visited by extraterrestrials.

PS

Yes, you were and again even those people are right. We did come and visit you, or rather we never stopped visiting you (for long periods). We intermingled with the Egyptians, who do you think helped to build the pyramids? Why, even today, your science cannot still do it with all its advancements in the technological age. We have always been on earth. Even today, we walk amongst you. Some see us and some don't and some look the other way, when they see us, through fear and ignorance they say to themselves "that cant be right, that's impossible, that's my imagination, that's not what I was told, I must be seeing things, or even worse they say to themselves, I must be going mad".

The Egyptians had two languages, not just one as you are told to believe and taught. They had two languages and they recorded details for the people of today in picture form/hieroglyphics as a message to pass down the generations. They tried their very best in order for the information to not become lost or distorted, but it has done exactly that. Much of the hieroglyphs are misinterpreted and misunderstood. We shall explain them to you. Are you ready?

The hieroglyphics are images of where you came from, different people came from different planets.

The Dog Star is an important one and its meaning is widely misinterpreted by your scholars. Different tribes, as you know them today, came from different planets. The Caucasians are a large race and have been intermingled much, but originally they came from different planets and are smaller in the number of peoples. They have grown considerably. It is not our concern. Races and creeds or cultures are not important to us. Let us be very clear on that. We do not discriminate one from the other, for no one is better than the other all are equal in our eyes.

The Ancient sites like Egypt we designed and helped to build, to remind people where they came from but this has been forgotten (as we knew it would), but we set in motion what needed to be done. We devised a plan to help people remember "who they are and where they came from". We did this all over the earth in several different places. Not all of them remain, some are lost.

That is why many of them "seem to" correlate to the stars. It is a map to show where they came from. You humans did not come from earth. Your history and science is inaccurate (some small parts are correct) but highly misinterpreted. And, therefore, it is mostly not worth bothering or concerning yourself with it.

We left a map on earth for you to remember who you are and where you came from. It is no mistake that the ancient sites correlate to the stars, we made it so. And yes, of course, Egypt is much older than you are told by science. The science that dated it is also now telling you it cannot be right, but in, the same sentence, it also says it cannot be wrong. So there is much debate going on, which is largely nonsense. Egypt often has an image amongst its hieroglyphics of a human with, different body parts, the real meaning of which is to record where humans came from, different planets. Some came from "the dog star" or Sirius as it's also known. The hieroglyphics spoke of where you came from.

CN

You do realise that I'm an uneducated woman living a simple life and so, who will believe these words. I had no knowledge of the Dog Star or much of Sirius, other than hearing the name, or of The Pleiadians either.

PS

Oh, but you do know much about us. We are right here so you can ask us anything and we answer. Do not seek out the information from other sources but get it directly from us. When it is written then you go and check it but do not check it first for it will cloud your channelling.

There is also a huge connection between Egypt, Atlantis, The Pyramids and The Crystal Skulls. Much has been hidden and lost on your earth, including ancient articles that contain knowledge like the Crystal Skulls and Atlantean crystal. Many books also and other sacred

250

artefacts/items/tools have also been lost. Huge healing temples have fallen into the sea that once held magnificent crystals, many of which today you could not lift without the use of machines.

Monday 22nd August 2011

PS

"We are the bringers of the dawn and we are the keepers of the dawn, do not forget that, you will find out what that really means. We are aware that you do not yet know what that means or the significance of it yet. It has much meaning and many complex truths are contained within those few words which have huge meaning and hidden truths within it. It contains secret knowledge of both the origins of humanity and us."

You know much more about Egypt than science. We have been guiding you since your young childhood. You do remember, don't you? {I do} then let us begin again. You have a great connection to Egypt, the land of the Pharaohs, the land of the Gods, our land. You even remember glimpses from past lives, don't you? {I do}. And we have shown you many great things about the land there. We have shown you what is under the Sphinx. You remember, don't you?

{I do} the time in your younger days when you were still a child, only ten years old {yes I remember so clearly, but I did understand the enormity of it} no, you were just a young child. Science is inaccurate and it plays a good game of falsehood and lies and deceit with humanity. It plays with you. Do not believe it. It is mainly nonsense but some truth lies within it. We showed you the Sphinx underneath and stairs that lead down, the stone steps, wide and long and magnificent. We showed you what lies at the bottom of the stairs lies a door to many great secrets and ancient knowledge and wisdom. These have been found and are being kept secret. Of course, they have, the great government have found them, found the secret chambers that lie there. The truth has been found already, my dear. It is being kept secret from you and all of humanity. It has been removed and kept in a highly guarded area. It is not in Egypt, it is in a place you call America, but we do not call it that. We call it the land of the wise.

We have shown you when you were ten years old the great connection between the Sphinx and what you call "Leo the lion" star system. Have we not? {Yes, you did} and you only recently saw that in the written word and it caused you to gasp for breath. Again, we say, don't believe your science, for it misleads you greatly. You know what the real truth is in your heart and again we say "pure of heart" for no falsehood lies within you. You are "pure of heart" and we love you, my dear child "we love you" so very much more than your own parents do. You feel that you know we shall bring you such joy, love, and comfort in the days that follow for you. We shall bring you your heart's desires. It will be our gift to you for opening your heart to us and allowing your self to open to us, for writing these words for us, for sharing with us, for communicating with us. We are so very grateful to you for allowing this whole experience to flow, for allowing it to happen and bringing it into existence and following through with it, for honouring it. We love you. You should never fear us, we know that you have in the past, but know that that feeling will lessen, so much so, that it will become non-existent and you shall rejoice at our being present with you. You will welcome us with open arms. And you shall see us, as you have the angels and others. In fact, you do already, and even right at this moment, you are doing so. Know that that "feeling" will only increase.

What we have shown you about Egypt is correct, all of it, the land, the Sphinx, the two languages, Leo the lion, all of it. Much more will come in time and you shall go to the land much sooner than you believe. You shall go there and place your hands on the stone and you will see great things that have not yet been shown to the people, to humanity, much is kept secret. But you have always known that {I have}. You shall write much more about Egypt later.

The Nazca lines you have been shown before {yes I have} during a meditation some of our brothers and sisters drew close to you, you remember, don't you? {yes I do}. And you were shown from the air that the lines were made from the air, that they were made by what you call extraterrestrials

CN

Were they made by you, the Pleiadians?

PS

No, we did not make them. Our brothers and sisters the Sirians made them, We are very close and share much as we are family. The Sirians are no different from us, they too love you and want to connect with you (Carol) and they will in time, for you will connect with them at a later date, but first "we" have much work to do. We said before and we say again, can you not feel them hovering in the background {yes, I can} and it brings them much joy, too. The Sirians made the Nazca lines from high above, again that was part of the map we left for you, to know the truth of where you came from. We are the ancient ones, we are the Gods, we are the ones you have been waiting for, we have been waiting for you, and you have been waiting for us. The time is now. Your consciousness is rising, humanity is shifting into the fourth dimension. And you know it is so. You know. You know the truth. Your vocabulary (man's) is very limited, so we keep using the same words and repeating ourselves for you to understand. Egypt had such a great language. In fact, it had two languages, one of which has been lost to the masses or rather it has been kept hidden from the masses. People do, indeed, know about it but even they are struggling to decipher it, some they understand, but a lot of it they do not. As we speak, they are trying to make sense of it.

CN

Wow, please slow down. I can't keep up with you.

PS

We had two languages and a few of your

scholars are examining them as we speak. The great scholars in today's world are trying to decipher it. Many of our books were destroyed at "The Great Fire of Alexandria". Again we have shown you that as a child. You do remember, don't you?

CN

Yes, I do…but who will believe me a simple, uneducated woman?

PS

You have the highest of education you have ancient knowledge. Nothing is higher or more important than that. Do not cry "Oh, Carol".

CN

I can't help it, I can't help it.

PS

Do not worry, the scholars will know the truth of what you are saying and they too shall contact you, albeit secretly. Your time will come; you have huge knowledge and wisdom. It shall be shared with your "science and scholars" For you have "contact with us" and the ancient ones, the wise ones. You have the secrets to all of humanity. What is wiser than that, we ask you? It is okay, we know you feel overwhelmed, you feel many emotions, due to our channelling this information. If you need to step back and rest a few minutes, do not ask our permission. Rest a few moments, pure of heart, you who have the wisdom, the ancient wisdom, that others seek.

And when the scholars, as you call them, come to you, do not fear them. Do not be afraid of their education and do not shy away from them. Embrace them as brothers and sisters who are just simply seeking knowledge, of knowledge they shall learn from you and they will be happy to do so. This will happen in America. You shall go there, also, and share your 'knowledge' with men first and then women afterwards. But the male scholars will come first from England, they will contact you. They will read "your book" and contact you first from England. That will be the start of it. Later on, in time, you will then go to America or rather you will be 'invited' by those men there and women will seek you out afterwards. It is extremely important that which you are doing now, writing these words that we "the Pleiadians" give you. Only, you do not realise the full extent of how invaluable the information is. And what's more, if you did, it would stop and hinder your willingness to, your willingness to engage so fully with us, as you are doing now. So it is best for you not to know the full extent of these words. It would stop you…this journey that you are on. You are not seeing the whole picture as we are, and know it, and that is for the best. But know that your day will come, when you will shine forth, you will go forth with your knowledge, with our knowledge.

Some of the large companies are putting large amounts of money into research. Much work is being done in secret and behind the scenes, largely in America but also all over the world. Many things are happening, in top secret buildings and areas, that are highly guarded. You do not need to know "too much" about these places yet. But we have shown you glimpses of them. More will come later.

Again, we say science is much more advanced than you are being told, by 'you' we mean the masses of people. Much of what is being done and has already been done in Egypt is being kept secret. The "scholars" are keeping much knowledge close to their chests.

Tuesday 30th August 2011

PS

The Two Suns

We are here, let us begin again. There will be a time when two suns (what will look like two suns) shall appear in your skies. It will come in your lifetime. Much has been written about it and even prophesied. It shall happen soon. It will be a spectacular event and one that goes against science as it is understood today by the men of science. It will happen over the next five years. And the people shall gather in huge crowds all over the planet to watch this happening, they will watch in awe at such an event.

CN

You cannot just tell me that, and then stop and not tell me more info, people will have many questions about that one simple sentence of yours.

PS

And so we shall but all in due course, the time will come later. It will all be an unfolding for you.

CN

J.S. has some questions for you.

PS

We shall get to that in a minute.

CN

Oh, yes, I remember and was stunned by it! You had electricity in Egypt. How can that be? It goes against what science says.

PS

Forget science. It is incomplete, as we said before. Do you just want us to repeat ourselves, or would you like to get new answers to your questions?

CN

I certainly would like to get "new answers" to my own questions. You know I don't have much faith in science, except for Quantum Physics.

PS

Okay, let us begin, again.

Electricity existed in Egypt. It lit up our walls and doorways, the great one with the two Pharaohs. We have shown you this as an image before. You do remember, don't you?

CN

Yes, I do.

PS

The image is correct of two Pharaoh statues standing outside an entrance. They were lit up by electricity that they held from their hands. We created electricity, we showed the great people of Egypt how to do this. They had electricity. It was taken from the earth. Many great men know how to do this today and in the past but they have been dismissed as cranks and pushed aside by others in power who didn't want this knowledge shared with the masses. For greed and corruption was in their heart. Energy/electricity was harnessed from the earth and used as electricity to light up Egypt. Do you really believe that such a great nation as ours which built structures and systems and temples that you cannot build today even with advanced machines and technology? Do you really believe that we had no electricity when we did all that? Do you really believe that a nation as advanced as ours was walking around "in the dark"?

CN

Well, when you put it like that, no, of course not, but science?

PS

Forget science. It is nonsense and you do know that. We know that you have much knowledge. Where do you think that comes from, Carol? We download it to you, mostly and it has raised your consciousness and awareness. Much more is to come. We have much to share with you and the world. We will keep "channelling" to all of those that are listening. Many are channels for us, not just you.

CN

You are answering my questions before I can ask them. Please slow down.

PS

Egypt was well lit up by electricity. It was harnessed from the earth.

CN

Yes, but how? I would like details specifically as to how you used the earth's energy.

PS

The earth has energy, in, of, and around it. We simply tapped into the earth's energy that lies beneath the soil and harnessed it for electricity. It has been done before we said. It is not new science. It is as old as Egypt. It was also used in Atlantis. Do you really believe that such advanced civilisations 'walked around in the dark'? Corruption and greed are stopping this from happening today.

CN

You keep talking about corruption and greed. I understand it and what you are saying. But to others, it will sound very negative? And I don't want that.

PS

So you want to control our words?

CN

No, I simply wish that you use different words and not sound so negative towards "powerful" people among the masses.

PS

Do not try and change our words. Write it as you are, as we give it to you. For that is a true channel. Let us help people to understand they are slaves to the system of power, greed, and corruption. You are aware of this and we know that fear creates fear. Let us help people with our own words, do not try and control them yourself. Just write what we give you and trust that it will be fine. It will *not* be taken as negative, but as the truth for it is so. It is the truth. Simply write our words and do not control them for that is a true channel.

CN

OK, I trust you. I really do. J.S. has some questions for you.

PS

We have been working with him also, for a long time and he has seen our energy. He *is* aware of us, he knows how tall, we are he has seen groups of us and our light shining in the dark. Both he and K.H saw our light shining, while there was a group of us. They saw this outside on the natural earth. The natural light was getting dark and they both saw us.

We have been working with him a long time and he knows it. There is much "stuff" that he keeps to himself and close to his chest. When the time is right, he too will share it. He is gathering a lot of information as we speak to put into a new book. He is simply waiting for the right time. He is much more aware than he lets on...he doesn't shine his light fully, while in the public eye doing interviews and such. He shares a little at a time so that people can accept this a little at a time...too much information for people would be considered to be "nonsense". It would be too much for people to take in all at once, and they would simply dismiss all of it. So he is correct in what he is doing in that sense. And he knows it and so does K.H. They walk gently at first.

CN
What is your interest in the people of the Earth?

PS

We are the bringers of the dawn. They are our children and we created them. We created humans, they are our sons and daughters. They came from us. They are not from earth and yet they are. But in the beginning, they came from us in our image. As we said before the word "God" in the Bible should be replaced with "Gods" not God. Yes, God does exist. But we are the ones who created you. And God created us. So both are true.

Some but not all of our children are like infants and at a very infantile stage, many are wise and we communicate with many of them. All spiritual teachers are wise. Much information is being downloaded and channelled but not all of it is from us, some is from God, guides and spirit people etc. There are many of "us", many star nations. We are not the only ones living in the universe. As there are many different humans, so there are many of us, from different planets and, yes, even galaxies, many different star nations. The governments know of our existence. And yet they keep it well hidden from the masses. Greatly influenced much through fear, fear that people shall rise up and know of their real heritage and beginnings.
People/humanity are being treated much like slaves and being kept in the dark.

Our interest in the people of the earth is our own interest for we created "them". We have been watching for a long while/time. And, yes, we did walk the earth, we laid the soles of our feet on the bare earth and walked and created you and then when we did that, we walked "with you". We lived on earth before you existed and with you.

We have much interest in you, you are our children. We are teaching you, albeit slowly. We are helping you to remember and wake up. We are helping you to raise your consciousness and, in doing so, we are with you watching your consciousness rising. We are assisting you to raise it. We are the bringers of the dawn. Again, we say, Carol, that the true meaning of those words will come forth and be known to you in all their entirety. They will. We teach, guide, nurture, aid and assist. But the governments *do know* of our existence and those like us. They know much is hidden. They know all about our existence on many planets, stars, and galaxies. And, yes, they are keeping you "dumbed down" for their own gain.

CN

I need a break.

PS

We will always be here for you. We draw close to K.H. She can feel us. She can "feel our energy and our love. She is not scared of us, she embraces us, with her heart for she knows the truth of us. She knows what we are about.

Now, let us get down to it, to the nitty-gritty, to the bigger picture of humanity and the secrets we told you about before, the secrets that are being kept hidden from you, that have yet to be published and they will, Carol. It *will be so.* We are here, we are the illumined ones, we are the bringers of the dawn.

CN

Yes, please, do get down to it, I feel that you are repeating a lot of words to me. I have many questions and feel that I need to hurry with this process.

PS

Yes, you are correct. Some of it you do need to hurry. You need to focus and concentrate your energies on channelling us, in order to be published. But not all of the information will come all at once. There will be a series of books from us and through us in the form of what you call channelling. And they *will be* received well and with open arms from the masses of people who walk among you. Many will buy the books, they already are aware of us and will delight that someone has written what they themselves already know to be true. And they will rejoice in the words. And they know the truth for they too have "seen" us. We walk with many. They will find comfort and solace in our words. Our words will help them to accept and believe more fully in their own experiences with us. We visit many. And many doubt. Our words will help them to accept, acknowledge what they already know in their souls to be true, but doubt with their minds, as they are taught to doubt. The true sense of real reality.

And yes we do live among you we dwell in secret places on earth. There are times when we come out and walk among you unnoticed for we blend our energy well so that our "light" as you would call it is hidden. Or rather so that we don't show our light, our essence, our spiritual knowledge. When spiritual knowledge is gathered in whatever race it shines forth for others to see. That is what you (Carol) see when you look at your teachers like the Dalai Lama, they do have an extra brightness around/about them, it is spiritual awareness of who they really are. And so do we, so we have to tone it down in order so as not to be seen and recognised by the people. For there reaction to us today would be fear, we are talking about the masses as a whole and not you individually. We walk with many, in the daylight. This halo has been shown above heads of saints and then misinterpreted down through the ages of man. But, in the beginning, it was not so.

CN

Have you ever had bases here on Earth in the past and currently
and what are the purposes of these bases?

PS

Yes, we had "bases on earth". We made a map of them. We came from the stars, as did our brothers and sisters from neighbouring planets like Sirius. The ancient sites that we lived in are many of the ancient sites which are still on earth but not all. Some are lost and have been removed and hidden from you. Egypt was one of the places, one of the ancient sites. It was a map on earth of where we came from within the universe. All of the sites we created and lived in were maps of where we came from, but not all remain. So parts of the map are missing or are hidden from the masses. The Sphinx has been recorded and told that it relates to "Leo the lion" and that is true, it does. There is much buried underneath the Sphinx and that is a mirror image of the skies beyond directly beyond/behind "Leo the lion". There is much to learn and many secrets in that place. All is a mirror of the secrets of the universe and where we came from.

CN

I need to rest and perhaps sleep. Please be here, dear Pleiadians when I come back I wish to continue right here, where we left off.

PS

We shall always be here when you call us forth. Always.

Monday 5th September 2011

PS

Are you refreshed?

And you remember your "dream". You understand your dreams better than most, you understand that they are real. Even the ones that are not, contain an element of truth or some solution to help people during their earthly existence and problems.

CN

Yes, I understand that. Come to think of it, I hardly actually "dream" at all any more. which is why most of my "dreams" seem real for they are. It's just that I'm in a different place and not in my body at all.

PS

We were with you during your dream. The dream state is a time when we and other "spirit/spiritual beings" are able to draw close to people, without fear of the rational mind, especially loved ones who have died.

CN

Can you just go straight to my "dream"? I know all that stuff.

PS

Yes, but others don't. Okay, we shall cover that later. The "dream" you had was real and you know much about how that process works. Let us remind you what you "saw" in your "dream". We were with you very closely. You are starting to fully welcome us with open arms and unconditional love and we feel that. As we said in the dream, we are "empathic" beings of light and we feel much in the same way that empathic (mediums/psychics) people do. It is just the same for us, only more so. For we do not have the human mind or condition or conditioned human mind. Those three things are separate and not always intertwined. They are separate, of themselves and exist independently. They are:

The Human Mind

Human Condition

Conditioned Human Mind

They are *not* always intertwined, as is believed. They are independent of each other.

Yes, your dream, let us continue then. The earth, the earth used to be much smaller than it is today. It has grown in size and become bigger than it used to be. It now contains vast amounts of water that were not there before in the beginning. You could have walked around the earth mostly on foot and not needed a boat to do so. Much of the land mass was joined together or very closely situated, side by side. The earth was thrown off course. It was impacted by a huge meteor this caused the poles to shift. Extreme weather followed and rain causing the earth to flood and swell, expand and contract. The oceans grew into vast masses of water, that simply were not there before. It created a huge flood on a global scale, the remains of which you can still see today on the earth. The oceans are but one example of the impact and changes, an impact of the "great flood". Many have occurred since that time. The poles did shift and they shall shift again. It is part of the earth's cycle of renewal. There have been numerous floods on earth since the beginning of time. You have seen the Sphinx with the markings of heavy rain etched into the side on pictures and you shall soon see it in the flesh. So it will be. Egypt is much older than science tells you. This has been rediscovered by science but it will not accept it in the mainstream, for science would then have to be re-written and explained to the masses. But that does not change the facts. It would also have to be re-written into science that because the Pyramids are, in fact, older than science has explained, that the Pyramids do in fact line up, align, with the stars from a much earlier period of time. That, of course, would also not be liked by science, as it would point out very clearly to the "scholars" that we came from the stars, though they do not wish to accept that, they, however, do know it to be true, but are unaccepting of the truth, for it would dismiss and affect their whole life's work. So you can see (Carol) why they are unaccepting, their *whole* lives work would be shown to be incorrect.

CN

Yes, I have never seen it like that before. Thank you for explaining it to me in that way.

PS

They are merely men, doing their best to explain science. But they have little or no knowledge or understanding of the spiritual laws, as you do. And, perhaps, they do not want to, for men of science who are "open" to receive knowledge and understanding in science, would surely find them. Look at Quantum Physics, that sure explains a whole lot and is a true science. It is a blend of Natural spiritual laws and science. It is united merely using different words depending on your viewpoint and where you are coming from, either from science or spiritual knowledge. Science is also changing though, it is going through a shift. Everything that you are is changing, there are huge evolutionary changes happening right now. And science is part of that. Nothing is separate from any other thing. All energy is part of energy.

Sunday 2nd October 2011

PS

Okay, let us begin again.

The ascension is happening and, in many of you, this is also affecting your brain power and causing it to increase. The more spiritually evolved you are the more it increases. The more you access the dormant brain power and knowledge. You exercise it at various times like a muscle, which it is. Not everyone is doing this but a large number of you who are spiritual have managed to increase your own brain power. Tests are being done, relatively new tests among "normal" people and spiritual people but the tests are not being honest about the reason for them. Everything about your bodies is changing, the chakras, the brain power, DNA, human consciousness, individual consciousness (of those who are spiritual and already at a higher level). All of it is changing among you. What is bigger than that? Your whole world is shifting and changing and adapting because consciousness is shifting up a gear or two or three. Ascension is very real. Only in hindsight will this be accepted by the masses who remain on earth and accept this journey (even if it is only accepted at a higher level). The earth is ascending and all those that choose to ascend with the earth will also do so, nothing on earth will remain out of balance or out of harmony with the earth. It is simply not possible, as it goes against the natural laws of science of the universe.

CN

Can you tell me where the new chakras are in the body, please? I had a message a week or so ago from you I believe, that we have new chakras, so can you be more exact about them and where they are in the body?

PS

We will list them for you with the older ones, which have increased in energy and got stronger. They are vibrating more so than before;

The Higher Crown

The Middle Crown

The Lower Crown

Third Eye

Lip/nose (between the lip and nose in the centre)

At the back of the neck in the centre (connected to the mouth so that the front of it is in the mouth/back of the throat)

Hypothalamus

Throat

Thalamus (between heart and throat) (or higher heart)

Heart

Sacral

Sacrum

Base /Root

Hips at the back. This is important for the ascension, as awareness increases in order to stay grounded while the ascension is happening, for the spiritually advanced ones to stay on earth, as there is such a great need for them. This is so much needed for them to stay on earth for the outcome of it all. They have a big part to play in the ascension process and must remain on the earth plane for it all to unfold.

Thyroid

Pineal and Pituitary *have got bigger*

Thighs

Knees

Calves

Ankle bone (just on the outside of it diagonally up a bit)

The foot chakras *have got bigger*

The auras have also increased in size and are becoming much stronger. They have increased in energy and got stronger. They are vibrating more so than before. The same is true for all energy whether its auras or chakras *all* energy is stronger. We will continue with the chakras later.

CN

My questions. Why are the ancient sites in the places they are?

PS

We will list them in a moment for you.

Stonehenge
Egypt
Easter Island is one of the places.

We will also continue with this at a later time.

November 2012

CN

It has been a whole year since I have written down your words that you have shared with me. Much has happened. It has been a very busy year for me.

PS

We are here, your frequency has changed and

improved. You now accept this as a normal part of you, more and more so.

CN

Yes, I do. Again, I have so many questions for you and you have been with me many times and I feel guilty that I haven't taken up a pen and written down all of the information you've shared with me. I hope that it will not be a whole year more again before my next time to write it all down, because I hear and feel your urgency to get this information out there into the world.

PS

You shall write more and more. Your energy system has been brought more into balance and alignment with ours. You've had experiences that cannot be explained by science or even some of your so-called mediums and spiritually aware people. You once had a meditation where we connected with you (I do remember it well, yes) and showed you the Nazca lines and that they were made from above the earth and yet someone in the group totally dismissed what you (Carol) were saying. We are saddened by that for it was her own logical mind and ego from where she spoke. We are truly sorry that you have had so much hurt and heartache. We feel your pain and anguish at it all and we know very well you are questioning yourself. With continuing your readings or just giving them up and completely focusing on your channelling us. You should continue with your readings, you have helped many people, much more than you know, continue your readings.

CN

Thank you. That means a lot to me because I was wondering if I should bother continuing with them.

PS

Yes, continue. It will get easier for you but it is important for you to stay grounded *you must* come into the forest and talk with us more. You will find it easier to connect with us there and we with you.

Your life purpose here in this lifetime has to do with channelling us, The Pleiadians and you know it (yes, I do) we have shown you much information and connected with you many times over the last year, even though we know and are well aware of your own personal journey, torment and upheaval but you have done well and we are most pleased with your progress. But for you dear one, you have to learn the art and technique of grounding yourself much more and better. Do so by going into the forest. You will be safe there with us, away from distractions and disturbances and from people knocking on the door and the telephone.

CN

I will, but I won't be able to write down your information when I'm there.

PS

That does not concern us. You shall remember it all later, we will make sure of it one way or another. You have done well and we fully support and embrace you for staying the course, many have not. Okay, let us begin from the beginning.

CN

But, I have so many questions for you, J.S. also has questions for you and I don't know where to start and *I'm* struggling with that.

PS

Just let our information flow and, maybe, put some of our questions on hold. This (Carol) is part of your life purpose that you contracted to do and we, (the Pleiadians), are going to make sure you do it. Our language is your language. We use your language (Carol) to get through to you. How else would we possibly get *you* to understand, if we used a foreign language, why, even 'You' would not understand it and that would be nonsense, so let the words from us flow to you.

CN

Okay, but many will disagree.

PS

Do not concern yourself with the opinions of others. If people cannot understand, it is because they are on a different frequency to yourself and that is of no concern to us. What is our concern is that people who are operating on a similar frequency to you will understand the truth of what we, The Pleiadians, are saying.

CN

I have very many questions, as I keep saying and I think it's spoiling the flow.

PS

We agree.

CN

So, I need some help here, please.

PS

Egypt. We helped to build the Pyramids, we have shown you much about Egypt…

CN

Please, hold on, I am finding my own questions and my mind is stopping the natural flow from you, I keep interrupting you and I can hear you laughing as I'm saying that. You have a good sense of humour and I do love you very much. Thank you for all of the experiences I've had with you from being a small, vulnerable little girl to the "dream" state experience/journey that you took me on last night.

PS

Egypt. In the beginning, God created us and we created the animals and dinosaurs. We created everything on earth with the help of the star nations that we are part of, as a family. Then we helped to build the Pyramids. The Pyramids are a much more complex structure than you realise. We talked before a little bit about it and now in more depth. The energy of the area where the Pyramids are always had a special energy. That is why we chose that area and other areas. There is a *huge*ly complex system of underground tunnels beneath the city of the Pharaohs and you well know it (I do, yes). We showed you that only last night more *clearly* but we have shown you many, many times until it sank into your everyday conscious awake and aware state. First, the energy of that place drew us, we then built the underground system for we knew what was to come, that it would be needed by people for shelter. We then helped the people to build the Pyramids on top of that area. This whole process took many years, for people are slow creators and many were lazy, even at that time.

CN

Really?

PS

Yes, it takes a lot of energy for Man to create

energy and movement and sound into reality, for us that is *not so*. If we wish to create something, it is done but, in your dimension, it is more complex and more difficult because you are operating on a more dense vibration and the more dense vibration something has, the more difficult it is to create something into being.

We used sound to create the Pyramids but man helped us. We created the Pyramids together and it took many years. It did not happen overnight. The Sphinx, as you well know, contains a lot of secrets that we showed you, as a child beneath the Sphinx (yes, I remember, it's still very vivid). On the back of the Sphinx, many ceremonies took place and we did land our ships on to the back of the Sphinx, as we have shown you. The streams of light. As we have already mentioned are one way we have of connecting with you and you remember this, don't you? (I do, yes and thank you). We are the Gods that created man with the help of other star nations. You on earth are taught many lies and yet you believe them. You are a very gullible species (we are, yes). All of the thirteen sacred sites on earth are a map of the stars and each of these places contains a special energy, though that energy has diminished a lot over the ages and that is why those places on earth were chosen. Each place is special to us and sacred, for we played our part in creating them from scratch with the help of humans.

Okay, you told me before that the number thirteen is very important and in more ways than one, but why?

PS

There are thirteen sacred sites because there were thirteen sacred tribes from thirteen sacred planets/stars that brought forth thirteen sacred crystal skulls. Do you see the connection emerging (wow, yes I do and I can feel the importance of what you are saying). Each crystal skull is embedded or encoded with ancient knowledge, each of them individually as to where they came from and the earths secret *true* history. The wisdom of the universe is contained in each of the crystals, individually, and yes there is a mother crystal that is in safe hands and will remain so, for now, that is until the time is right and ready for it to emerge. Thirteen is also sacred in geometry and that is also important within this Universe that we belong to. There were also thirteen separate places that each tribe went to settle and each tribe built a large complex structure. Not all of these structures remain and that is why you can only list eight of them. The others should remain hidden for a little while longer we say for a little while but our time is much different to your time on earth. For us, time is much quicker than yours. Humans and the star nations helped to create these structures together.

CN

Please, list the sites for me and others reading this

PS

1) Egypt

2) Stonehenge

3) Atlantis

4) Peru

5) Sedona

6) Lemuria

7) Easter Island

8) Acropolis (underneath the new buildings is sacred ground upon which we The Pleiadians walked)

One of the other sacred places is hidden beneath the ice in the North Pole. That will be found and come to light when the Poles shift again fully.

The thirteen tribes settled on earth but they did not come from earth. We created man in our image and then we interbreed with man and woman and we found much pleasure in this. The Ancient Indigenous peoples, the thirteen sacred ancient tribes came from us, the star nations, and settled upon the earth.

CN

I need a break. This is hard going for me.

PS

Conscious beings are not limited to the earth in the form of humans. There are many places in the universe that contain and have life forms of intelligent light beings with and without bodies as you perceive them. Energy is universal. It is not confined to earth. How arrogant and old that way of thinking is! The Universe couldn't hold its own if energy *only* existed on earth. It would be a huge imbalance and go against the natural laws of the universe. That would be an impossible and *nonsense* situation. It just does not exist in the Universe. The Universe is pure energy and earth is *part* of that, not the other way around, not the way of thinking that the earth is the only place of energy (human beings).

CN

Back to Egypt, please, because you are way ahead of me!

PS

Egypt and the Nile, the path of the Nile was changed, its course was changed many aeons ago. *No,* do not change our words. We told you before (okay I'm sorry I did correct it though) and we are pleased you did so. We again say to you (Carol) do not change a single word, keep it as we say it. This is Your life mission or part of it, so do not worry. You *will* have time for all of it. We love you but you need to slow down and not rush, even though you *feel* our urgency to get this information out. Do not rush or change it. Keep it as it is and don't worry. People will understand for we are not talking nonsense as science does (oh, you are funny, I like your humour) We do mock science too. Where do you think you (Carol) get that feeling from?

CN

Well okay, I get it…because from a very young

age, you have shown me the truth and certain experiences...and...

PS

And it was us, The Pleiadians, that kept you (Carol) away from the school system because we *knew* that it would distort your life purpose, because it would instil into you *huge* untruths, even though, at the time you didn't fully understand that, but you do now (yes, I understand it much more now and again, thank you). We needed you (Carol) as we needed all of you that are helping in this great evolutionary shift of humanity. A New Dawn has begun and you should all rejoice, for it truly is a magnificent time for you to be on earth (at this time). And the Poles have shifted even more since you wrote last year.

CN

I remember I was shown a quarter degree shift in the Poles from North to West. Was it you who showed me that?

PS

Yes, it was us. The crust of the earth is changing. It is again breathing new life into the earth and shaking off the old ways that no longer serve her. Mother earth is going through a birthing process and is being purified once more. Part of the planetary alignments and changes that are happening are all part of this. *For everything that exists is interconnected in a huge way.* We feel that humanity is now getting that and understanding it more and more and more, in a more complex way, or getting to grips with it more and understanding its depth.

CN

You have kind of moved away from Egypt and I wanted to stay on that subject I know you have so much to say about Egypt.

PS

Yes, you are right. We do, but at this time we want to talk about the changes coming because we feel that it is more urgent. Egypt can wait a while for she is not going anywhere. She survived the last pole shifts and will survive this one, too. Humans will not all survive unless they adapt to the new energies with those that are emerging. Humans DNA is changing. Human bodies are changing, nothing in the Universe is separate from anything else, so when something as small and beautiful as a human body changes *all* parts of it change. The human energy field is changing, its awareness is shifting up a gear or two or three or four depending on what level it is on. (You, Carol are on/blending with the fourth dimension, soon to be in fifth) but you will all be on the 5th when the time is right and you will all do so at much around the same time. But our times are different and to you human time is longer than for us. So, when one part of the human body or awareness changes, it all changes, hence the chakras change. The aura changes and expands, the mind/brain begins to use more of itself, everything about humans expands and increases and becomes more aware, both individually and globally, because *you* are all connected by an energy source as we are, too. This energy source can be *read* by many people that you call psychics and mediums. In fact, you have many names for them like sensitive, empathic, clairvoyant, many, many names but it all means much the same thing. You/they are simply reading the energy source fields of the person or the place or whatever it is that you're reading. Everything is energy and when you do readings or mediumship or connect with us or even with God, it is simply that you are connecting with and reading this energy. Sometimes, the connection is so mild that you only get it unconsciously and cannot describe it fully, because it hasn't integrated into the physical, but we are working on that.

Humanity is changing and because humanity is changing *we,* The Pleiadians, and other star nations are changing. Earth humans think they are the only ones going through the huge shift of consciousness and waking up, it is *not* the whole universe is expanding and becoming more and more aware, even us! We, too, are also evolving. Humans will have to adapt again, as they did before during the last pole shift and planetary alignments or else they will not survive. But the whole point of your being here (Carol) and many, many others like you is to help with the process. We know you are eager to move on, so let us do so but, first take, your five minutes, if you need to, we will wait for you.

CN

Thank you. The Indigos, Crystal Children, Rainbow Children, please explain. I know you have already but please do so again for people reading these words

PS

The children you describe are part of the star nations. They have spent time (being) with us. That is why they are more sensitive to energy, more psychic, more empathic, feel things more and each one, in turn, has been. And is more aware than the ones that came before. The ones that came first, the Indigos in the sixties and seventies find it the hardest to adjust and live in this world where things are so dumbed down for you. The ones that are still coming in now are finding it much easier but they do so, only because the first ones paved the path for them, so to speak. Also, another important point to make is past lives with these beings, we mean with each other, is now being remembered by humans collectively. So, yes, when you (Carol) remembered being with Claire (name has been changed) it is correct. You were with her on the planet/star system.

CN

Okay, Thank you for sharing that with me. Why is it that when I'm channelling you and actually writing it down, I need to keep my energy levels up, I find they drop so much. You know I already have a low blood sugar level. I try to avoid sugar as much as I can but I love chocolate.

PS

We are glad you mentioned this and will cover it very briefly for now. Energy needs energy to sustain it especially people who are psychic or in any way sensitive. There are many names for them, including the children we mentioned above because of their heightened state of awareness. In order to explain this, we will change the word awareness into the word "energy", so people who have more "energy/awareness" need more energy *especially* when channelling so that in order for you to hold the energy/vibration, more energy needs to be released and in order for you to do so, you, need more energy, hence food sugar is one of the sources to do it quickly. Also, what's important is that when you're channelling us and similar star nations, our vibration is very high so you will naturally need more energy within the body to do so, to bring your awareness up. Awareness is connected to the brain and food. How could it not be? That's another misconception or one that is largely *overlooked* anyway. Let us move on. If need be we will go into depth later on. Let us return to the Indigos you mentioned. And, as you said, (Carol) you remember Claire being on the Pleiades and you remember knowing her from there. That is also correct, as was Atlantis. You've had a few past lives with her.

CN

Oh, my Sugar!

PS

Sugar, children love sugar and sweets and cakes and part of the reason they do so, much is because they are largely Indigos/crystals/rainbow children. These children absolutely *love* chocolate and all sugary foods because they raise their vibration and give them more energy, more spiritual/psychic energy, and experiences, though it is very bad at the same time. It does have a huge impact and effect on the brain, as well as the nervous system! Many of these children have been misdiagnosed with ADHD and other conditions, which is incorrect and untrue. It's just that your Doctors don't know what to label them, so they had to come up with a new label for the new children. Many of or most of these children are very sensitive to their environment and surroundings, both in a good way and a bad way. They "pick up everything" around them, whether it is good or bad. The bad things can and do have a negative effect on them, causing them to overreact and go into overdrive, as they struggle to handle the situation and are often unable to do so. However, the good positive things, as you see them, cause them to be very peaceful and relaxing, almost in a blissful state, that seems somehow unnatural to their families around them and that sometimes also causes a concern. So these new children are misdiagnosed and given medication that they should never be taking in the first place. But, even this too, will change as you evolve. During the shift of consciousness, it will all unfold and make sense in the long term. But it does go a step further than that, the powers that be (the negative ones) are well aware of this and of who these children are and that they are here to help humanity shift during this process of evolution. So it is their aim to dumb them down with medication and that is exactly what they are still doing and have done since these children began to come into earth's energy. That, too, will soon change. It cannot, not.

To Be Continued............

Depths of Life/Crystal On The Ocean Bed

Crystal On The Ocean Bed

Far Beneath The Deep

Depths of life, wild force and untamed

Deepest blue, black, brightest star

Lies its soft belly upon the ocean floor

Untouchable and silent,

Silently waiting for the day to end

When it shall be found in the year 2012

Crystal clear, blue ocean covers a million
thousand secrets, that lie buried and covered
over

In a milky white haze

And the gulls cry louder still for never a nation will
set us free.

Upon the ocean bed, we lie silently waiting in
nothing,

nothing but stillness and silence. Our waves
wash into the shore, in and out never ceasing

Cascading and caressing the sand and toes of (human) man.

Whoever will find us laying in the stillness shall be a lucky soul

For he will reap the fruits of our gold,

Spiritual Gold,

That is worth

Priceless Gold of infinity and murky depths

We lay upon the ocean floor in silence waiting, waiting to be found by the spiritual man who seeks

Spiritual Gold and it shines crystal clear like an emerald jewel

long since forgotten by the conditioned mind.

Huge temples lay flooded and bare, drenched and soaked in waves and depths of despair,

A race, a nation were we

At the beginning of time, temples of immortality. The truth of our origins are out there

Somewhere upon the ocean floor, warm and cold. Like ice, we share emerald jade crystals

Huge as the mountain stone,

Jagged and polished shining freely for all to see, yet not found, unknown to some and unbelieved by many,

But still we wait to be found and our find shall change humanity

For they will cry "It cannot be so, oh, let it not be true, Oh, let it be true"

Oh, let it be true. Let my origins shine through to my soul, that I shall remember,

Remember who I am and where I came from, from the stars that I gaze upon

Let my soul be known, let our souls be known, my brother and sister forever immortal

In what is known as insanity, in the human society, that today we know as civilised and just

Let it be so, let it known for all humanity to see

That we are one, you and I, that there is no difference

When I look at you, I see myself and a thousand words unspoken, a thousand wars, all crying "no"

In a cage of civilised humanity and slaves for them

"Kings may enforce Heaven's commands on Earth, but Shamans travel to the sky and consort with the celestial gods in person"

E.C. Krupp

Chapter 13

The Present

Bitter-Sweet Taste

November 2012, in spite of all my experiences, I have not ended up bitter and twisted, as you might imagine someone who has gone through what I have, I am not one of the statistics. It's probably because I am spiritual that I am not one of the statistics. I don't hate my abusers, I'm not filled with hatred towards them.

The prisons and mental institutions are crammed full of people like me, who sadly, have had similar childhoods. Without these spiritual experiences, I wouldn't be here today. Quite honestly, I don't know how people survive those kinds of childhood without the spiritual worlds, I know in my heart that I wouldn't have. *And I would like to Honour them here for they are truly Heroes.*

I still believe in God and the natural order of the universe with all its faults, for they are not faults at all. It's how you perceive them, that they then become faults, but they are not. They teach us what we need to learn, to experience. They give us exactly what we need to grow, to learn, to experience, to grow spiritually. Therefore, we should welcome them with open arms. It's in our darkest hours that we have the opportunity to grow the most *if* we choose to. In experiencing the worst situations in our lives, if we grow from these experiences, we can become our true authentic selves more, that we are meant to be. Everything is the way it's meant to be, even the really awful things. There are *no mistakes, ever.* God/The Universe is working to its own natural divine Law. It is the Pure Divine God energy, neither male nor female but both and it is never wrong. For us to understand that is also part of its great lesson. We are also part of it, not at all separate. So, in truth, at a higher level, we already know the outcomes of everything that is and will ever be, with that I leave you. In God's name see the magic that you really are. Do not continue to be conditioned. Let go of it, let go of the material world and experience all that is God.

Oh, Lordy!

Oh, Lordy, I miss my mum. I miss the mum I never had. I miss those few rare moments when alcohol was far from sight and nowhere to be seen or *smelt*. Those days in Dublin at the zoo, the smell of the trees and nature, the sounds of the birds around, the sounds of the peacocks in the distance, unseen but well heard. I miss those rare moments of peace and tranquillity when all was well. I miss the mum I never had, the mum that others had. I miss the mum I should have had, the mum she could have been, the mum she must have wanted to be, the mum she herself must have longed for. Mostly, I just miss my mum. Guilt is such a small word but plays heavily on the heart.

The Last Christmas

Christmas is once again creeping in, bringing back all those memories and with it cravings, longings for the perfect Christmas card surroundings, of family and love, warm fires, stockings filled with love, armchairs and cats, sleigh bells, church bells, as the choir sings and rejoices for the family waiting at home, warm food awaits - roast turkey, mulled wine and mince pies that melt in your mouth, sweet cherry pies that my mum used to make. The only thing missing every year was everything else, all the above. So once again Christmas is creeping in as I write these words, as well as all the memories that I try to forget, every year. This year brings with it an ache that lies out there somewhere, I hope.

Not surprisingly, Christmas is and has always been the hardest time of year, for me to stomach as it brings the full realisation with it every year, the realisation of mum being an alcoholic and with it, her *need* to put that first; before all of us or even before *any* of us. My poor old dear mum, when she passes to the world of spirit, she will remain an alcoholic. She is seventy-eight and still clings to the bottle, her body old and withered, her mind unable to just simply let go.

What emotion and memories lie beneath the bottle for her. Is the pain too hard for her? I feel it must be so. Why else? What else? I feel guilty, guilty for being born on the same day as my little brother who died, many years before me, buried in a joint plot of poverty, the insects eating away at his tiny frail body. He died in his pram outside, slowly choking to death in the smog, Lee, my oldest brother, survived, who silently sat next to him in the pram, Lee being only a year older or younger. It has just dawned on me that my mum must forever hold that memory and associate it with Lee. How could she not? Some deep unconscious part of her must also blame Lee, or rather jog some part of her that associates Lee with that memory, and myself as I was born on the same day that he died and passed to the world of spirit.

It all brings back a realisation I had a few years ago of how guilty and responsible I felt, throughout my childhood, for my mum's addiction and, therefore, lack of everything that the addiction brought forth with it, lack of love, lack of food, nourishment, warmth, encouragement, a "*safe*" home, warmth and clothes. And still she will die that way, she cannot stop it would (I guess) open up the floodgates to her emotions, which I assume she cannot cope with.

So, another Christmas comes for me again this year and stillness. Every year, I plan to be in some hot far off place, far away from the memory of the past. I still long to escape those emotions. With every Christmas year that comes, they become less and less. One thing that has stayed with me since those days, is Hope.

The Wounded Healer

I was first told when I was between ten and
twelve by The Pleiadians that I would someday
write and they encouraged me to start it there
and then and I did. I listened. I was told that I
would someday write about all of my experiences
and the spiritual laws, knowledge that I'd been
shown. I began to write this book when I was
between ten and twelve. I forget which but
remember the first sentence began "My childhood
was an unhappy one". What an understatement
that was. I only remember the words so well and
the whole situation as my brother found my
writing and read it in front of me. He was
questioning me and my "unhappy childhood" by
reading my words back to me and the look he
gave me had a big question mark at the end of it.
I couldn't believe it, he was even asking me why
he had lived with us and witnessed the craziness
of my mum and the way she was. He'd had a
glimpse of some of the abuse from the men he
pulled off me or beat up after the fact. I thought it
was sad, funny and stupid that he would even
ask me; Why I had an "unhappy childhood"? But
looking back, I understand it differently, I now see
that he was really hoping it wasn't true. Even
though he knew it was, some part of him was

only hoping and wishing for the best, seeing the world through rose-tinted glasses.

Much of the abuse I experienced is *unknown* to my brother, sister, mum and family, as are many of the spiritual experiences, especially the Pleiadians. For many years I was introverted, quiet, shy, subdued but I was also happy in that world that I still share with my guides and helpers. My brother and I remain close, we spoke a few years ago about it. He spoke freely to me of that time, explaining that he knew I was in another world, but couldn't understand why or where I was. It's called the spirit world, which is why I was thought of as autistic or similar. Nothing could be further from the truth. I feel he accepts my psychic abilities, mediumship and spiritual awareness, at least I hope and pray that he does. Though we don't often talk enough on the phone, we are still close and I know in my heart that we have shared many lifetimes together, some I have witnessed but not all, not yet anyway. He has often been my "protector", though I have never spoken of those to him or with him. I sadly think he would be dismissive of them, so I don't, I just *feel and know* that the bond between us is very strong. We come back to what/who we know and love. We are eternal beings, there is no death.

These days I am happily working as a psychic, medium, and healer, though I am just beginning a whole new chapter in my life and my story doesn't end here. It is only just beginning for me. My path as a Shaman, I embrace it. Often, when I think of those years, it feels to me like a distant nightmare, one that is fading with time, more and more so. Anyone who has experienced trauma will also experience nightmares or the "sweats", whether it's a war-torn experience or not, those nightmares that I *used* to get often nightly. They didn't stop happening until many years after the facts, they only stopped in my early twenties. I know that I will never, ever experience those nightmares again. A huge weight has been lifted from my shoulders, one that will not never return.

It brings a sense of peace, freedom, and courage that I have somehow managed against all the odds and statistics, stacked so highly against me. I was born into a nightmare. Only for the Grace of God, Jesus, Archangels, Ascended Masters, Star Nations, Ancestors, The Spirit World, my Spirit Guides and Helpers and my much loved The Pleiadians who walk with me by my side. I would not have survived. It is only for all of them that I continued to walk this earthly path and remain in my body. Without Jesus and them, I would not be here today. I would have taken my own life, without anyone knowing why and the abusers would have been free and ugly to roam and prey on innocent children. I honour them and this is part of that honour, love, and respect, it is not for me. Releasing this book is also very much part of my life purpose and in doing so, I release the past, more and more, for a New Dawn is coming both for me and all of humanity. It is time to shed the old and just let go of it. To my dearest brother whom I have never told just how much I love him, we are blood. To my family that I was born into, may God bless you and love you and keep you safe, away from all harm, may he be there for you, may he give you all that you couldn't give me. May he hold you in his light for all eternity. I love you still.

Wishing on a Star

I wrote this in November or early December 2012.

Christmas is looming, drawing close and creeping in once again, but this year it feels different. My story doesn't end here. These are just some of my memories of the trauma, the spiritual realms and the Pleiadians that got me through and kept me sane. Without them and the spiritual experiences I had as a child, especially the one with Jesus, I would not be here today. These memories are from zero-sixteen or rather seven-sixteen, as far back as my memory has allowed me so far. Before that, I still have little memory of anything, due to more abuse and blocked memories. I know I also experienced much more abuse before the age of eight. My memory has blocked it out. Quite honestly, today, I don't know whether I even want those memories to come alive and be re-born into my eyes, my visionary field of consciousness. Because, if they come back then I will have to deal with them, too, and at this moment in time, my feeling is more excited about the future. In writing of this, I've had to go back and remember many things in order to be able to write about them, I wrote in my own words, as I experienced each and every situation, as a child. I had to relive it, as I wrote it, in order to remember it. I just want to let go of it all. I'm done with remembering unless it's the Pleiadians, or it involves them. I don't think it serves me, any more., to look back, I'm tired of the past, I've faced it, and most of it, I didn't like what I saw or experienced.

I cannot explain or describe the words I have or the love I have for spirit, Jesus and the

Pleiadians, who are my family of light beings. And without them, I would just be another statistic, without any hope, disregarded and lost, soulless. My love for them I cannot describe. The English language only has two words for love; Love and beauty, and those two words don't come anywhere near what I feel for spirit or my love for them.

The English language only has two words to describe love but there are very many different kinds of love. And yet hate and anger have so many more words to describe them. Our Language and vocabulary are really very limited. I know there was a time when our language was rich and contained more, a lot of it has been pulled from us at the time of Atlantis. A whole lot of things were distorted, destroyed, hidden and kept from us. *But the Veil is being lifted.* And each of us has a part to play, we are cosmic beings having a physical experience here on earth. We are not the limited beings we are told or conditioned to be. Each of us is Divine.

My sister always said to just "forget it, forget the past" but I wasn't made that way. I had to live it, breathe it, unearth it, rebirth it, remember it. My family were, are, so good at sweeping everything under the carpet. All I could see was a huge pile of stuff building up, causing blockages and chaos. So I had to deal with it, so I could heal it and release it and, *Finally,* let it go. And considering everything, I think I've done okay.

My sister learned to bury it, my mum turned to the bottle and my sister turned to food, as I once did, I once turned to both food and the bottle. Perhaps it's better that those memories before seven remain buried forever? Only time will tell. And only time heals.

Doors are being opened for me at this time in my life. Rather it seems that all of my life, and its different varying chapters doors, have been opened and many opportunities given, not always in clear, obvious ways. That are now only making a whole lot more sense to me. The hundreds, if not thousands of spiritual experiences I've had, are only beginning to make sense to me.

Writing has also helped me to see a clear picture emerging. Though they are not taking me into a direction I'd planned, hoped or envisioned for myself, It seems I have been called to be a Shaman. This isn't something that I would ever have chosen for myself. It has been a very difficult, not one to be chosen, the path of the wounded healer. But I have made my promise to spirit, one that I will honour to the end. Part of my own journey begins in America or Canada, I'm being pulled but I don't know how the events will unfold, but I know my feet will soon, once again, walk the lands and soil of the Americas, and with it part of me, more whole, more complete, more fully integrated. It is in that place that I shall/will become more at one with mother earth and father sky, Aho.

Father Heaven, Mother Earth

Father Heaven, Mother Earth,

Spirits of the Ancestors,

Tanger of the four directions,

Ongom Spirits,

Nature Spirits of the Mountain, Water, and the
Sea

Spirits of all animals,

I honour you and thank you.

Please be watching over me,

Please help me Hurai, Hurai, Hurai,

You stand before me and behind me,

At my right and at my left,

You are above and below me Hurai, Hurai, Hurai,

Follow me like a flock of birds,

You have called me to be a Shaman,

Put the vision in my eyes, the words in my mouth,

Give me the power to become a Shaman Hurai,
Hurai, Hurai.

Om maahan, Om maahan, Om maahan

Maggalam.

The Gift of Death

My mum died on Boxing Day at eight minutes past ten in the evening in 2013. I had arrived at about nine pm, just time enough to see her, say goodbye, just enough time to help her into the spirit world. She was scared to go, she wasn't just scared, she was terrified of it, she didn't know for sure what lay there beyond and was in a state of panic, she was clinging on to dear life, out of fear of what lay beyond for her.

I had a call on Thursday six days before she died from my brother Mark in the UK. I knew as soon as he called me, I knew that she was going to die and did not have long, but I didn't tell him that I knew I couldn't, not until I saw her. I was trying to give him time. Spirit had kept telling me, for at least six months previously, but I kept ignoring them, I couldn't face it, I didn't want to hear it. But I knew it was coming and death kept creeping closer and I kept running from it, trying to drown their voices of spirit out, telling them to go away, let me be, let it not be so. I avoided it at all costs, much to my own peril. For I had knowledge from the world of spirit as to what was to come and I could have done something, maybe, but I didn't, I couldn't face it, I hadn't the strength, the voice, or the courage. I become deaf to spirit when they told me and I kept them at bay, not wanting to hear them, or listen. I turned the music on full volume and sang my lungs out, stilling their voices of death and sending them back to heaven where they belonged. With their faces hung low and sadness in their hearts, they left me in stillness, but they still always came back to repeat their words. They wouldn't let it rest and I couldn't hear it, I covered my ears well for about six months to a year. I became deaf to them.

But the call still came and I had to face it, there was nowhere left to run, except into the arms of death.

My mum's death brought a grief I didn't know I had in me. It shook me to my very core, I had never experienced grief like this, *not ever*, not even when my Granddad died, whom I loved dearly. But children deal with grief so differently. When I cried, I couldn't stop and I sounded like a wounded animal howling, howling for its mum. I got down on to the floor and melted into it, retching my tears of grief into the earth, always alone with the privacy to let it all out, to let go, to let it all rip without judgement, without shame, and I could only do that alone but not without guilt.

Just the previous week, I had done my Shamanic course on "the weekend of death" and I knew, every part of me knew that they were related, I could feel it in every part of my body. My being, my soul, my cells even knew and I was okay with the two being related, but I was not okay with my mum dying.

I took the coach and spent a few days with her, not wanting to leave her side. I arrived at the hospital. At my first sight of her, I saw a beautiful, frail old lady, who was yellow and jaundiced. My breath left me and tears started to build, tears I had promised I wouldn't let her see. Part of me didn't want her to know she was dying. But, as ever, my face said it all, I've never been able to keep expression out of my face or eyes and the one time that I longed to do so, I couldn't, I knew she saw it in my face and she could see it in my eyes and it made me cry even more. She said little to me except "Hello and thank you for coming" and one or two negative comments. But I just wanted to grab her up from her chair and hug her, hold her tight and squeeze her and tell her how very much I loved her. But she looked very frail, very fragile. Had I done that, I felt like I would have broken something. So I didn't, I just sat in the chair looking at her. I spent the whole time, half in the spirit world talking to them, at the same time as talking to my mum. She knew she was going, just like my poor old granddad did all those years before. She herself was half in the spirit world and half in this one.

I had to go home as I had work on Christmas Day in Galway so I took the coach home. I stayed for the day, relieved to be home, to have my own, much-needed space. I was preparing myself for her death and packing clothes, black clothes for the funeral when spirits arrived and, this time, I called out to them. When I arrived back in Galway, as soon as I was just getting off the coach, I had a call from my cousin to say mum had taken a turn for the worst. I knew I had to go back. I was to help my own mum into the spirit world. I needed courage and strength and I needed a day (at least) to prepare myself, gather my courage and strength and call my guides in. I would need them like never before, not only to deal with, and help her pass into the spirit world, but I also needed their help, love, courage to deal with my stepdad, who acted like he had never abused me. And I had to play along, as far as he was concerned. I couldn't raise that ugly elephant in the room, not at the time of my mum's death. But I still had to look at him, pretending like nothing had happened, with him pretending and voicing to everyone that would listen, how horrible I was. He had made me out to be a bad person, and that he was the victim. His being in a wheelchair only added to everyone's "oh poor Del story". My mum was dying but I had to help her, make her journey as easy, as painless as possible, or rather I wanted to, needed to.

The day I spent at home in Galway I prayed for her constantly, and talked to her constantly, as she was half in the spirit world, I knew she could hear me and she answered me. I begged her to wait for me, to let me help her, I begged her constantly, with a grief I never knew I had and it shook me to my core. I will never feel grief like that again, I hope. In all of my thirty-nine years of being a medium, nothing could have prepared me for it, for all the emotions that I had came like waves, I could no longer hold them back. But I had to, at least for a while. I had a job to do of helping her into the spirit world, I was honoured to do so and very humbled by it. It left such an effect and impact on me, that it even changed how I work as a medium. I thought I had understood grief, but I was wrong, I had known nothing at all. But I do now. I had a job to do as a medium and help my mum into the spirit world, and the part of her that was already in the spirit world knew this and we spoke much. The part of her, the part of my mum that was already in the spirit world, finally understood and accepted me for the work that I do. I could feel Love emanating towards me for it and it brought a fresh set of tears from my eyes, because she finally, finally, on her deathbed, understood and got it, and accepted it. But God why did she have to wait so long? Why did she have to wait until now?

The day my mum was buried, the day of the funeral will never be forgotten in my memory. It was one of the most painful days I've *"ever"* known. The death of my mum was a gift, as strange as it may sound. It was a gift, a release for her, for me, for both my brothers. It released her spirit, her pain, both physically and emotionally. It released me, it released both my brothers of the past. It brought closure to an immense amount of suffering for all of us, for different reasons. She had given us a gift of death and release from the past. We all felt it, both me and my brothers, words were shared between us, of the cruel, cathartic gift of death. A connection was shared and felt between the three of us, a connection of family ties, of blood, of kinship, of what we had experienced, seen, witnessed, been exposed to, often at the cruel hands of our mum and her painful addiction.

During the days of my mum's funeral, it seemed her spirit was to taunt me, to haunt me through my aunt Mary. It was such a cruel hand of fate that I simply couldn't believe it. It stunned me into the silence of disbelief. My two brothers arrived at my aunt's house the night before the funeral. I was starving, but not thinking of food at all at such a time. They came in and sat down at the dining room table, where she offered them beef stew. She had known that I was really hungry as I'd casually mentioned it, trying not to be rude. She dished them both up a delicious beef stew as they sat down side by side, hungrily eating away and talking few words. I stood around not knowing what to do with myself, feeling very deflated, there were only two chairs at the table so I couldn't even sit down. My Aunt Mary was refusing me food, as my own mum had done, at the time of my mum's funeral. I was speechless but I left it alone as I didn't have the strength for confrontation. Mary knew full well what she was doing. It was like my mum had come back from the grave to taunt me with food again, except she wasn't even buried yet. I was distraught and this just added to my pain. Was there no let up in my mum?

It happened again. Twice the next day, the day my mum was buried, once in the morning and then in the afternoon/evening. It caught me unaware and showed me quite clearly just how much dysfunction is embedded in our family. I "never" felt more separated from them. The incident in the dining room the night before. It dawned on me that my aunt Mary had purposely set up the dining room table arrangements for only two chairs, for both my brothers and not me. She was well aware of what she was doing, consciously creating a divide between me and my brothers (or at least trying to do her up-most to do so) separating, dividing and taking sides. I couldn't believe how cruel she was being, except I was experiencing her cruelty, her cold-heartedness, it was all aimed at me. I felt like a wounded dog that was being kicked in the heart of the wound.

The morning before the funeral I was even hungrier than the night before, and running on empty. Mary was still refusing me food so I asked my cousins husband to drop me at the nearest shop/garage in his car, as they lived in the middle of nowhere and I didn't drive. He is a lovely guy and was quite happy to offer. So off we went, I didn't buy very much, only a pre-roasted chicken. When we got back to the house, I went into the kitchen to get some plates. My plan was to share the chicken with everyone, to sit down and eat with everyone. However, that didn't happen.

My aunt was in the kitchen when I entered it. The vibes I got from her were not in the least bit friendly. She did not welcome me or the chicken.

Suddenly, I didn't feel very hungry at all, no doubt because of the stress of it all. I shared some words with her about having bought a cooked chicken, if anyone wanted some. I started to leave the kitchen. As I was doing so, the chicken was very quickly put away protectively out of my reach. Her meaning was that I couldn't have any of that either. To me, it really was quite unbelievable, as I had bought the chicken myself. Again I let it go. At this point, hunger had left me and I no longer even wanted the chicken. It was never mentioned, I didn't see it again. When I went to get some later, it had gone without a trace or a thank you.

On the afternoon/evening time after the funeral, after much alcohol and only a few sandwiches in the local pub, I'd drank a huge amount with both my brothers, except I wasn't used to it and they were. In fact, for about two weeks, I was rarely without a glass in my hand.

We arrived back at the house me, my Aunt Mary and my cousin. We left the pub earlier than everyone else, wanting space I guess to be alone. On entering the house, my aunt stated that *"there was no food in the house for me"* as she turned to my cousin and asked her to feed the small dog. A little while later, the rest of my cousins arrived unaware of what had happened. They made pizza and did offer, but I refused.

I'm still reeling from it, even today. This has been the hardest memory to write, although not the most painful. But it's the rawest and I *still* haven't had enough time to heal from it. All my other memories I've healed from and had time to do so. This is still raw and painful and the hardest to write, to remember. I haven't seen her since then and have no desire to see her again. It's over, I will no longer allow myself to be treated that way. During the funeral and my mum's death part of me stepped back into victim mode, which is why I didn't stand up to my aunt and say anything to her. It came to me afterwards that she had taken Del's side and made it clear to me that she didn't consider me to be a victim of abuse. The dynamics were really ugly. I want no part of it any more.

It *feels so good* to get this out of my system, to acknowledge it, to acknowledge the way my Aunt Mary treated me, because my family, especially my two brothers couldn't handle it, couldn't deal with it, and wanted to avoid it. I am not going to deny it, I'm going to voice it, here in my writing. That's just how dysfunctional my family are.

The death of my mum brought back everything to me, painful memories of my forgotten childhood that lay buried, of my real father and the bruise that he caused me physically. It shook up old "stuff" of past hurts that resurfaced for me. Sometimes, it seemed unbearable. Memories came back to haunt me again, feeling like I was re-living it all over again. I didn't know what was happening to me, but then I realised I had post-traumatic shock syndrome. Once I knew what the problem was, I knew it could be healed, which I did with the help of Shamanic healing, spirit, and friends.

When a parent or abuser dies, it is very common for post-traumatic shock syndrome to occur (again). It can be a trigger for memories to resurface again, it can seem overwhelming, but it can be healed, as with everything.

The Café

I sat writing away in a café in Galway when I felt my mum come in from the world of spirit and draw close to me. She kindly shared kind words from her heart. It seems she has evolved and learnt some, since passing to the spirit world. I became a channel for her words and simply wrote what she said, as she said it. It brought a fresh set of tears to my eyes, even though I was writing in public with people around me, who were watching my tears, I didn't care, I needed to cry and let it out.

"My daughter, my dearest, kindest daughter Carol. I know I was cruel and I am so sorry, my dearest daughter, please will you ever forgive me for the heartache I caused you? I let you fall by the wayside. I abandoned you long ago, I have learned much since my death, and seen how wrong I was. I love you so very much, please, dear Carol, forgive me. My heart is open *now* like it never was when I had a physical life. Now I see how wrong I was and the hurt I caused you. But *now* I truly do love you, with all my heart, like I never could and never did, when I was here with you on the earth. I love you. You brought forth a pureness of heart, an awareness I never understood, my heart was so closed then. But it is so different now and so open. Go forwards in your life and know that I'm here on the other side helping you and I love you so much, so much more than I ever did when I had life in me. America awaits you and I'm helping you to step into your true self, your true voice, your true path.

There is much talk amongst us in the spirit world of you, your path, your future, and the greatness we know you are going to achieve; more forward, even if it's slowly, move forward at a gentle pace. You have much more strength and courage than I ever had, you're a lion of strength, untamed wild and free. Sweet child of mine, you."

The strangest thing is as I'm writing your words Mum, in a café in Galway, upstairs and outside in the fresh air, smoking away, a table near me with three females. Are all having a conversation about their own father, who lies dying in a hospital, as you did, due to alcohol, as you did? Many times since I was young I've had strange conversations and overheard them too and this is one of them, which seem and feel to be part of a much bigger picture. The universe really is a mirror and every day, more and more, grows stronger and stronger. It mirrors itself/myself back to me. In the strangest ways, in the most beautiful ways and sometimes in the most unbelievable ways, it does so.

I still haven't felt ready to connect and talk to my mum in spirit, even though it has been over two years since her death. She has come to me and spoken to me, like the time in the café and she was very much around at the funeral. But I was more of an observer, just watching and listening to her, not wanting to fully engage in a conversation *"with"* her. I feel I'm ready and willing now to open up and have a relationship with her, the kind we never had when she was alive. I've always known that I would be able to have a much better relationship with her from the world of spirit. I very much look forward to giving her some time and space to talk, to connecting heart to heart with her.

Some years ago, while living on Holy Island in Scotland, spirit showed me an image, a vision. They showed me that God is like the ocean and we are like the individual droplets of water. Much more recently, spirit has shown me why grief can be so painful. The closer we are to someone the more essence/energy we contain within ourselves of them. (We contain the secrets of the universe within our selves.) if you have two or three droplets of water together (or a whole family of them) and one dies the other two will feel immense pain of loss, of grief as if part of themselves has died because it has. It all comes down to energy, particles, matter, molecules, atoms. Humans are all connected, no matter what the space or time difference in-between, which is why molecules will react in the same way, regardless of the distance or space in-between.

Afterword

All too often, we put spiritual people on "pedestals" and, all too often, they fall off. I've done it myself and been hurt by it. It is a lesson. I've also been put on a "pedestal" myself. It was a great lesson to my student of my humanness. One of my best teachers is always reminding me of his own humanness. We are all human, including and especially "spiritual" people. We all have our own lessons and trials and tribulations in life, our own failed relationships, our own traumas, our pasts, our sadness, death, grief and life experience. We are human beings, simply just more aware. We still have our foibles and sins, for none of us is perfect. Yet, we are all perfect in the eyes of God. Being spiritual doesn't make life easier, it can and often does make it a lot harder, trying to squeeze ourselves into a world that doesn't understand us and our "frequencies", can often set us apart, as we are operating on different "frequencies"; oil and water simply don't mix.

In truth, there are no mistakes. Our experiences are meant to be, however difficult they are, or may seem, however painful, or traumatic. If we can see the lessons in them and often the bigger picture, we can choose to grow from them or not. This is ours alone. We are in charge of our own lives, but not always the things that happen to us (at a third-dimensional level, at a human level). Bad things do happen to good people, it is a chance to grow spiritually if we choose to. Our experiences make us human. If we understood (as a whole) that trauma can bring such beauty, it would cease hatred. If we understood (as a whole) that war only breeds war, it would stop us in our tracks.

My writing this book brings some closure for me of my childhood. It is closing one door and opening another. It has and is taking me on a journey, an amazing journey of my connection to The Pleiadians and things continue to unfold for me all the time. I have *much more* information to channel from them. In fact, I have a very strong sense of "knowing" that this is to be part of my life's work and mission. I am extremely blessed, but sometimes it seems to me as if I've come from somewhere like Auschwitz and then won the lottery.

Droplets

We are all connected like the roots of a tree. We come back to who we know, to the people and families we know, to the places and spaces we know. It is our familiarity and love of those that draws us back. We all have memory (even if it lies dormant in the unconscious) of past lives in different places far from our homes. We remember places and languages we do not speak nor have learned in this lifetime. We are all connected. To do harm to another is to harm ourselves and vice versa. Spirit (and energy) is universal. It has a collective and an individual consciousness. It has memory, it is a living, breathing thing. Our cells have memory, everything that lives, that has life, has memory, even if it is unconscious. Sometimes this memory wakes up and we remember who we are and our past lives. Trees have memory of ancient times and contain within them the history of the earth stretching far back into the past, out into the universe, of the galaxies, of everything.

The oldest tree in the world was found some years ago in Africa. It was then cut down by the same man to see how old it was. Perhaps, if he had known how simple it was/is and with much less effort on his part, he could simply have asked the tree itself how old it was. In the silence, we can find answers to our biggest questions within the universe, about the universe. We do not need PhDs or doctors degrees. All we need to do is so much simpler and takes so much less effort and energy. All we really need to do is connect with nature to mother earth. The earth is not dead. It has life, plants and trees have life energy and contain medicine. We have everything we need, without machines, drugs or technology. We have lost our way, it's time now to find it again. There is nothing special about me. I'm just another pebble in the ocean. I don't have a Ph.D. or a doctors degree I had little formal education. One thing I do know about is the spiritual laws that govern the universe, energy and how it works. If I can connect with The Pleiadians and star nations, *"we all can"*.

Appendices

Evidence that dinosaurs walked & lived at the same time as Man.

www.ancientexplorers.com/blogs/news/proof-of-humans-and-dinosaurs-together
www.answersingenesis.org/dinosaurs/footprints/human-and-dinosaur-footprints-in-turkmenistan/
www.apologeticspress.org/APContent.aspx?category=9&article=4664
www.archaeologicalworld.blogspot.co.uk/2012/07/nile-mosaic-of-palestrina.html
www.archaeologyexpert.co.uk/earlyfootprints.html
www.creation.com/human-and-dinosaur-fossil-footprints
www.creationevidence.org/carlbaugh/v2ch1.htm
www.creationmuseum.org/
www.creationtruth.org/
www.creationwiki.org/Talk:Dinosaur
www.genesispark.com/exhibits/evidence/paleontological/footprints/
www.oldearth.org/argument/D111_creation_science.htm
www.paleo.cc/paluxy/russ.htm
www.rae.org/essay-links/tuba/

www.s8int.com/
www.s8int.com/dinolit2.html
www.s8int.com/dinolit25.html
www.s8int.com/phile/dinolit56.html
www.s8int.com/phile/page66.html
www.scribd.com/document/35103936/ANATOMY
-OF-AN-EXPEDITION-Dinosaurs-Central-Asiatic-
Expeditions-and-Diaries-of-Walter-Granger-or-
WALTER-GRANGER-AND-THE-CENTRAL-
ASIATIC-EXPEDITIONS
www.talkorigins.org/faqs/paluxy.html
www.visioninconsciousness.org/Ancient_Civilizati
ons_39.htm

Space Archaeologist Uncovers Ancient Egyptian
Ruins

Sarah Parcak is an Egyptologist and
Archaeologist who has used satellite imaging to
discover and unearth Egypt's ancient settlements,
pyramids and palaces lost in the sands of time,
that Psychics, Mediums, Mystics, and Shaman
have been talking about for years!

www.sarahparcak.com

Details of the Thirteenth Star Sign

Capricorn:	Jan. 20-Feb. 16.
Aquarius:	Feb. 16-March 11.
Pisces:	March 11-April 18.
Aries:	April 18-May 13.
Taurus:	May 13-June 21.
Gemini:	June 21-July 20.
Cancer:	July 20-Aug. 10.
Leo:	Aug. 10-Sept. 16.
Virgo:	Sept. 16-Oct. 30.
Libra:	Oct. 30-Nov. 23.
Scorpio:	Nov. 23-29.
Ophiuchus:	Nov. 29-Dec. 17.
Sagittarius:	Dec. 17-Jan. 20.

About The Author

Carol Noonan helps in finding missing persons and has previously worked with the police in Ireland, UK, and USA. She has appeared on My Spirit Radio and Westport Radio in Ireland. She has featured in Prediction Magazine in the UK, The Sun and Woman's Way in Ireland. She has been interviewed by Bill Peters on the Slice and Maarteen Horst on ET First Contact Radio, which can be viewed here

www.youtube.com/watch?v=3ERRlgn0J_8&t=1114s

www.youtube.com/watch?v=ittzuyZkrqk&t=1608s

www.youtube.com/watch?v=kTBT5me9RKY&t=544s

She offers courses, training, talks, workshops & events, Pleiadian talks, in Ireland, UK and internationally. She is currently based in Portsmouth, England and offers a range of services for individuals and groups, families, in person, online and internationally via Skype. Attends Psychic Fairs in the UK, Ireland, UFO talks internationally, book signings, charity events and online webinars. To see a full range of services and to get in touch please visit any of the following sites:

www.thepleiadianchild.com

www.facebook.com/thepleiadianchild

www.facebook.com/carolnoonan

www.linkedin.com/in/carol-noonan-114a53131/

www.twitter.com/carolnoonan

www.youtube.com/user/noonancarol

Email: thepleiadianchild@hotmail.com

If you have read Carol's book please leave a review at Amazon.

If you would like to receive videos, updates, discounts, and more then you can sign up to Carol's newsletter at www.thepleiadianchild.com

Carol Noonan, aka "The Pleiadian Child", is in the process of setting up an International School/Retreat Centre: "The Pleiadian School of Light". If you would like to donate/help or participate, your help will be greatly appreciated.

Please log on to www.thepleiadianchild.com or www.facebook.com/thepleiadianchild

Made in United States
North Haven, CT
15 December 2024